THE TIMES

careers & jobs
in
travel and tourism

The TOURISM SOCIETY

People in all the right places

verité reily collins

KOGAN
PAGE

First published in Great Britain in 2004 by Kogan Page Limited

Kogan Page Limited
120 Pentonville Road
London N1 9JN
United Kingdom
www.kogan-page.co.uk

© Verité Reily Collins, 2004

The views expressed in this book are those of the author, and are not necessarily the same as those of Times Newspapers Ltd.

British Library Cataloguing in Publication Data

A CIP record for this book is available from the British Library.

ISBN 0 7494 4205 0

Typeset by Saxon Graphics Ltd, Derby
Printed and bound in Great Britain by Clays Ltd, St Ives plc

Contents

Contents

Forewords

The Tourism Society is delighted to be associated with this publication, especially as the author is a long-standing member. Now that tourism has become the most important industry worldwide in terms of employment and income generation, those seeking to work in it need all the help they can get. Sometimes, as the Society's recently engaged Meetings Executive, Flo Powell, MTS, states below, choosing to work in tourism may not always be the obvious career path to follow. In my case graduating 38 years ago with a BA (Hons) in French, it was definitely not the obvious choice for me. As it turned out, my whole professional life, working primarily for the UK's tourist boards (BTA, LTB and ETB) and latterly for The Tourism Society, has been singularly rewarding – if at times frustrating and even annoying. But then, any worthwhile job is just like that.

Adrian Clark
Director, The Tourism Society

TOURISM – A CHOICE CAREER

The tourism industry offers flexibility, choice and involvement in one of the largest and fastest-growing industries in the world. There are more tourism courses available than ever before at different levels, and more people are realising that tourism is an industry they can see themselves working in for years to come.

Like most students in sixth form, my choices for further education were made on a bit of a whim. I was doing a GNVQ in Leisure and Tourism and an A-level in Psychology and came to the strange career choice of criminal psychology or tourism. Being 18, I opted for Tourism mainly because I wanted to travel the world and get paid for it! I chose a BA in Tourism Studies at Bournemouth University because the course had an excellent reputation and it was by the sea. Tourism sounded like fun, and I still wasn't entirely sure what I wanted to do 'when I grew up'.

Studying Tourism gave me room to learn the mechanics of business and offered the choice of a number of sub-sectors. In my first year I was interested in airlines, in the second it was sustainable tourism development and during the third year I discovered a sector of the industry I hadn't given proper consideration: event management. I worked for International Students House in London for my third-year industrial placement and thoroughly enjoyed myself. Having had this wonderful experience, when I graduated I began seeking out jobs in this sector and was pointed in the direction of The Tourism Society, where I now work as Meetings Executive.

Flo Powell
Meetings Executive, The Tourism Society

Introduction

IS THIS THE JOB FOR YOU?

Ask yourself:

- Do you have good health and stamina?
- Do you get on with people?
- Do you have 'stickability' – are you determined to finish a job?
- Are you able to work shifts/at weekends/perhaps away from home?
- Are you able to support yourself while you get started? Some top jobs in travel require a start-up period before you are earning good money.
- Are you cheerful whatever the weather and time of day/night?
- Do you suffer unduly from travel sickness?
- Do you speak business languages? These can be very helpful.
- Do you like reading? You have to research for many travel jobs, not rely on the Internet.
- Given the name of a 'new' place, are you curious to know more about it?

Still reading? Then you probably have what it takes to work in the travel and tourism industry – in many countries the most important source of jobs.

But you have to be able to handle change, and the whole industry is changing out of all recognition. Twenty years ago the package tour two-week family holiday was the most important element in travel, but some risky companies gave the industry a bad name. Ten years ago, the EU Package Travel Directive came in to force, which gave travellers protection, provided they had bought a package including two out of three elements:

1. travel;

2. accommodation;

3. services (car hire, ferry tickets, etc).

Then came the World Wide Web. Browsers discovered unlimited possibilities if they used the Internet to book their own travel, and now individually booked holidays are the fastest growing sector.

Thanks to the Web, low-cost airlines selling on the Internet rather than via travel agents are now opening up around the world – founded by hard-nosed business people who couldn't care less about the romance of flying, but know how today's marketing techniques entice passengers into filling their planes and keep them flying profitably.

Thanks to the Internet, clients think nothing of booking hotels halfway across the world. They may never have seen them, but believe Web photos. Once at the hotel, there is no tour operator's rep to sort out problems if the hotel doesn't come up to expectations, and they discover they are on their own. They can't complain, but shrug and think, 'Better luck next time'. And there will be a next time, as travel has become relatively cheap.

Today's visitor is apt to question tourism's over-development. Spain, previously an enthusiastic high-rise hotel developer, has begun to tear down its concrete hotels and complexes and become more eco-friendly. Even conservationist and TV presenter David Bellamy has gone on record as saying that sensitive tourism development can be the saviour of many countries – so things are looking good on the conservation front.

Post-Concorde, the luxury market is looking for 'new' and more luxurious services to entice high-spending customers. Short-break holidays catering for special interests are gaining in popularity. Adventure holidays, winter sports, more affordable long-haul destinations, weddings abroad, and the rise in low-cost airlines and their knock-on effects all encourage consumers to travel.

Entry

Obviously the more skills and qualifications you have, the better, but the industry also wants enthusiasm and 'stickability'. Many people come into the industry working as representatives, and these qualities are important: enthusiasm is needed when working long hours. 'Stickability' means persevering with a problem until you have sorted out whatever has gone wrong: hurricanes, strikes, bad weather, delays, etc.

Today, many staff are hired for their expertise and experience. Good news for mature readers! Women returners and staff with experience are particularly welcome in the industry; the business travel sector relies heavily on people with the maturity to deal with demands from time-poor cash-rich customers. There is virtually no gender discrimination, although there tend to be more women heading conference organisations and more men at the top in tour operations, and lots of theories to explain this!

Travel and tourism is one of the largest industries in the world, but it can be difficult to find your first job as the industry is principally made up of small companies, with few major household names. Many companies started on the kitchen table; thanks to the World Wide Web you can work from anywhere – and people do. A lot of companies have started out with someone offering a service a big company doesn't provide, and built up from there. Niche marketing, offering holidays to a certain section of enthusiasts, is increasingly popular; there are still many gaps in this sector, waiting for someone to start up a business offering different specialist tours.

Getting started

- Be flexible.

- You must have stamina – and 'not-so-common' sense.

- A sense of humour is a definite plus.

- First Aid knowledge is important.

- Strategic career planning should be something you do automatically, rather than waiting for things to go wrong.

- Take courses to increase your knowledge, skills and qualifications (even if only a one-day seminar).

- Be optimistic!

Job opportunities

You just can't ignore the rise and rise of the tourism sector around the world. However, today's customers are better informed than ever before and old-fashioned tourism providers averse to change are receiving fewer visitors. Opportunities are there for anyone prepared to be proactive and deliver what the customer wants, rather than depending on the 'old-style' tourism ethos that people would buy anything as long as it was cheap.

New trends

- Airlines increasingly offering 'extras', and passengers looking for cheap business and first class deals on the Net.

- Better hotel rooms. It is almost unthinkable for a hotel to provide a room *without* a bath.

- Forget the hotel swimming pool – luxury hotels have to offer much more, including genuine spa treatments.

■ Rise of short breaks – at the expense of the traditional two-week holiday.

■ Enquiring tourists who genuinely want to know how locals live, and see more of a country, rather than lie on the beach all day.

■ Cruising is increasing in popularity.

■ Allied professions such as hospitality, aviation and leisure show increased bookings.

Salaries

Salaries are still low in most sectors, although they are improving for middle managers and above. Perks help make up some shortfall, and companies are realising that if they don't pay good wages, staff vote with their feet and go to work for a rival.

Invest in yourself

If you are serious about working in the tourism industry, the best way to find jobs is networking. You may find this difficult to do – but if you aren't keen to get out and meet people, how can you persuade a company that you are able to work in tourism, an industry where you are in constant contact with strangers?

A good place to start is at Tourism Society meetings, where you will meet potential employers. If you are worried you don't know anyone, offer to help hand round eats, check in people, or distribute leaflets. If you have something to do, it is much less frightening the first time. If there is nothing to do, go round and ask everyone if they could tell you what their company does, especially if they are standing on their own. They might be new too, and would appreciate someone to talk to. Tourism is a sociable industry, and many jobs are offered to someone met at trade functions.

The Tourism Society is an all-embracing group of top tourism professionals, where you meet people at functions from across a wide spectrum. Members include some of the more progressive tourism lecturers, eco-warriors with their heads screwed on, pragmatic company bosses; in fact a fascinating cross-section.

Languages

Although English is the language of tourism, it is still important to be able to speak the language of countries and people with whom you are dealing. It is better manners, and gives you a commercial advantage. There is a worrying trend for Europeans to be headhunted for top UK jobs, because they speak a range of languages. You don't need to speak like a native – just enough to carry on a business conversation.

Which language? As long as it is one that is used for business – almost any one. Not an obscure dialect spoken by no one outside a small valley, but European languages, especially Spanish if you wish to work in South America (and Portuguese for Brazil) are useful. Russian is also becoming more common and the opening up of the old Silk Route could make Turkish a viable language. Arabic is extremely useful, and it is said that within five years China will be the force to be reckoned with.

Disabilities

It is illegal for companies to discriminate against job applicants and employees because of their disabilities and there are many career and job opportunities open to people with disabilities within this sector. A good information source is the Disability Rights Commission Web site at www.drc-gb.org, which provides accessible information relating to the Disability Discrimination Act.

1

Tour operators

THE EMPLOYERS

Tour operators put together package tours for holidays or business trips, either to sell to the public, or to act as wholesalers who put together packages which they sell to coach companies, overseas companies wanting a tour in their country, newspaper readers' offers, etc. These companies then sell the tours to the public.

A package usually consists of transport, accommodation and services such as reps, transfers, etc, which clients buy as inclusive packages from travel agencies or direct from the tour operator.

Tour operators can be small companies working in one area, perhaps offering special interest holidays such as family holidays, self-catering, cycling, walking, cultural tours, visiting cultural and historical sites, sports or adventure packages, etc. Alternatively, they can be large companies, sometimes employing several thousand people, offering a range of holidays for singles, couples, families and older clients, all over the world. Many major operators have bought up small specialist companies and still operate under these names, knowing clients will think they are having individual attention.

> *TIP*
>
> If you like going on holiday with a particular company, ask if they have vacancies. If you are 'their' type of client, there may well be a job for someone who understands their ethos.

The UK tour operating industry is split into three separate sectors:

1. The largest sector is outward-bound holidays sold to the British public, who want a tour abroad for their annual holiday or for a short break. Generally these companies will be members of ABTA (Association of British Travel Agents) and/or AITO (Association of Independent Tour Operators):
   - 60 million Britons went abroad last year;
   - 39.9 million were on holiday, 20.1 million on business;
   - 20.6 million took package holidays, around 90 per cent with ABTA member companies.

2. Incoming visitors from overseas to the UK. Companies looking after incoming visitors are generally members of BITOA (British Incoming Tour Operators' Association) and/or members of the appropriate regional tourist board. Most people have heard of the giant tour operators that send British clients abroad, but this incoming industry is a huge sector which in 2002 looked after 24.2 millions overseas visitors:
   - 32 per cent leisure (holiday) traffic;
   - 30 per cent business travel (this is the most rapidly growing sector);
   - 26 per cent VFR (visiting friends and relatives).

3. Companies operating domestic holidays for British people in the UK, ie canal boat operators, coach tours, weekend breaks, etc. Other companies such as Butlins, Pontins and Center Parcs are not tour operators in the strict sense of the word, but provide employment for thousands, and work almost totally with the domestic market. Then there are individual holidays, especially day tours, where visitors make their own arrangements.

In total in 2002 there was a turnover of £76 billion from domestic and foreign tourism, of which:

■ £15 billion was income from overseas visitors;

■ £26.7 billion was from domestic visitors on short breaks or main holidays;

■ £34 billion was from domestic visitors on day trips.

THE JOBS

Work in a tour operators' office means working at a desk for a large part of the time, but you also get to travel, visiting venues, checking hotels and restaurants and trying out sightseeing tours.

If you are good at design and planning, there is work in the brochure planning departments. Product planning is another department, and you will be expected to review sales, quality and profit performance of the current holidays. You also assess market conditions to plan programmes that will offer a good holiday to clients, from which your company will make a profit. Marketing and management experience is always useful in these jobs.

One of the most important departments is the finance department; margins can be so tight that fluctuation of the pound against the euro by a per cent of a point can make the difference between profit and loss. Work in this sector generally involves travel, as you have to visit outlets. The contracts department works very closely with finance and accounts, planning one or two years in advance what price to pay for hotel rooms, chartering aircraft, etc.

Then there are IT departments, legal (very important), customer relations, marketing, product development (finding and researching new areas and ideas), maintenance (for villas, chalets, campsites, etc), public relations, reservations and call centre staff, etc.

Although there are some very large tour operators, the majority of companies are small, and often do not advertise job vacancies. Jobs often go to those already working for the company, or who know someone working in the company.

Tour operators are usually members of ABTA or AITO, and abide by the EU Package Tour Directive and by a code of conduct that covers matters such as procedures in the event of alterations, cancellations, surcharges or overbooking.

TIP

Many people start work as overseas representatives and work their way up the company career ladder.

Clare Simpson

Starting as a rep, Clare Simpson was promoted to Resort Manager, and now she is Area Manager, based on the Greek island of Kos. If anyone had told her she would enjoy working 24 hours a day, she would have thought they were mad! But, supervising the resort staff while waiting at the airport for a delayed flight, she realises she gets a buzz from helping people, even though conditions can be dire. When the flight finally arrives it makes all the difference when a family say to her staff 'Thank heavens you are here.'

Luckily delays don't happen too often, but Clare has other problems to sort out, from the lads who think they can take the local drink – then get horrible hangovers – or the couple who were so excited on a boat trip that the woman dropped her handbag into the sea, and there were complications with getting replacement traveller's cheques. Then she has major problems when a hotelier says he has to close off a complete floor because of flooding (caused by one of 'her' passengers), or the local ferries decide to go on strike, cancelling all the excursions to Rhodes and other islands.

Three years earlier, sitting in a classroom on a training course, she never thought she would actually be living in Kos, sharing a flat with two girls – not that they ever seem to spend much time there. Her tutor had egged her on to apply to her company, but all she could remember of that awful interview was when she had tripped and landed in front of the interview panel – and the rest of the day had been a blur. Afterwards the senior rep had told her they were so impressed when she picked herself up and laughed, they decided to accept her almost immediately.

Her parents are coming on holiday next week, and she can't wait to take them to a taverna for dinner, then up to the olive groves where her mother can pick wild herbs for her cooking, and they will probably end up at the company Greek night in a famous restaurant. It is great fun, especially when everyone dances a conga around the tables. But for the moment, she has to make her weekly report. Did she say she enjoyed her job? Well, most of it!

For the future

Many people are looking for newer and more interesting activities during their annual holiday, especially sports and fitness. Sometimes these turn into ideas that are the start of a new tour operation. Mountain biking is one case in point: there hardly seems to be a mountain that doesn't have a bike track used by groups of holidaymakers. Taking sports further, there is a rise in companies going in with a charity to offer a 'challenge' to holidaymakers: cycle the Gobi Desert, ride the biggest waves, camel trek across the Sahara or whatever, as a way of raising money.

The major tour operators are constantly on the lookout for ideas to encourage people to book. Once operators sent families off on holidays to hotels, then someone discovered self-catering. Mothers decided it was easier to keep an eye on children and their food if they could cook the family meals, and so the giant self-catering tour operations started.

Teenagers couldn't wait to break away from the family and go on holiday on their own, but actually didn't want to be on their own – they wanted to be with others of the same age group. So holidays catering for the 18–30 age group started. At the opposite end of the spectrum, 'Golden Oldies' holidays started.

Saga Holidays

One specialist operator is Saga Holidays. Sidney de Haan bought a hotel in Folkestone in 1948. Wondering how to fill it during the winter months, he offered special terms to retired visitors. The one-week all-in package for around £6 was a tremendous success, and he found he had hit on a unique formula. As people live longer, so there are more 'over 50s' – Saga's target audience. Now the company is valued at £1 billion.

When you think about it, the list is endless. The giant tour operator Thomson has just purchased a company offering up-market cottages for holidays. Then there are sailing, painting, activity holidays... Activity holidays are the fastest-growing sector of the families market; families with pre-teens and teenage children find they can do the activities together – and have fun. Other activity holidays set out to stretch the fitness and ability of clients, particularly young couples, who love the challenge of para-gliding, sailing, canoeing, kayaking, dog sledding – the list is endless.

Almost every time someone thinks up another holiday activity, it seems a small company starts up to handle bookings. Sometimes it gets big – or is taken over by one of the major operators.

Reps make contacts during their work abroad. These contacts can be used if they decide to set up a tour operation, and many do. From holidays for bee-keeping enthusiasts to historians who want to visit battlefields, someone has set up tours to take these people off to indulge their interests while on holiday.

So when you are working, don't forget to collect business cards, telephone numbers and ideas; this will give you the nucleus of your contacts database.

Michelle Ramsey

Michelle Ramsey had always been interested in TV programmes about travel and far-away places, and decided a career as a rep was the job for her.

Starting with a distance-learning course for representatives, she applied to companies from the list that came with her course. After a number of replies she had an interview with Airtours, and 'within 10 days I was sent to Corfu'.

She moved companies several times – this is normal in travel as many jobs are in small companies where there is no chance of promotion until someone retires. 'Eventually I became Senior Head Rep and then in 1996, Resort Manager for a newly formed holiday company.'

During the winter she worked for the Tourism Training Organisation, training reps, guides and staff for jobs in the travel industry. 'Companies such as Kosmar ask us to organise in-house training for their staff, so life gets hectic during the weeks before Easter when the season starts.' She organises and speaks during seminars run to give people an insight into jobs in travel: what types of qualifications and skills are needed, what are interviews like, what do the jobs actually entail, etc.

Training usually finishes in April, at the beginning of the summer season, and starts again in October. In summer, 'I work freelance for different companies as a Tour Manager for European and North American tours; I enjoy the variety, and this keeps up my industry knowledge.'

Career progression was basically down to training. 'I take as many courses as I can and whenever I go for an interview, companies are always impressed to see people wanting to better themselves; you can never have too many qualifications. When I assist in recruiting for companies now I always look for those people who hold a useful qualification. It shows they are serious about working in our industry.'

She has met up with a colleague who runs an incoming tour operation. He is looking for a partner to expand his operation, and they will probably go into business together, he providing the clients through his contacts, and she booking hotels, air flights and services through her contacts.

GETTING STARTED

Under 18?

Most companies ask for entrants aged 18 or over. And no, it's not because they think you can't handle the work, but insurance companies often won't insure people who are under 18 for work outside their country.

So what should you do if you're too young? Fill in the time with projects and/or a job that will look good on your CV and give you experience of dealing with people:

- work in a fast food restaurant;

- work in a shop;

- help out with pensioners;

- work with young children;

- help a charity such as RNLI, Age Concern, Save the Children, etc (read the GNVQ intermediate textbook for leisure and tourism, which describes working on a charity flag day; see pages 242–251);

- ask your local leisure club/swimming pool if they need staff;

- help out with a local environmental project;

- take a job as an au pair through a reputable agency that gives you support and assistance while you are working with the family;

- help your local Scouts or Girl Guides or similar youth organisation;

- look in your local papers for details of local tour operators and coach companies offering tours. Ask if they need any Saturday/part-time staff.

Plan to take suitable courses for the two years between 16 and 18. No education is wasted in tourism – but everyone's career path is individual to them, and in tourism if you are sensible you will take job opportunities and courses as they arise (see Chapter 13 on training):

- take an NNEB or Level 3 NVQ in Childcare;

- learn or perfect a language;

- take a course at a local college – phone the Travel Training Company (see Chapter 14) for details;

- take a holiday reps course – phone the Tourism Training Organisation (see Chapter 14);

- learn bookkeeping at your local college;

- ask if your local adult education college offers language tuition. You could also try history or dance classes – Spanish dancing, belly dancing, etc – anything that will introduce you to the culture of other countries where you want to work;

- ask your local museums and public art galleries if they have any lectures to teach you about the culture of the countries where you want to work; they will often have special low rates or even free entrance for under 18s.

When you are 17 and six months

■ Start applying to companies. You may be too young for some, but take note of what they say, learn from this, and it should help you to focus on companies that will give you an interview.

■ Don't expect to be offered a job from your first interview. You will be up against people who are older, and most companies will want people with experience.

■ Regard each interview as a learning experience. Listen to what the interviewers say – this will help you with your next interview.

■ It is always useful to write back to the company when you receive a 'No thanks' letter. Thank them for taking the time to give you an interview, mention something positive that you liked about the company, and say that if they are looking for staff in the future you would like to be considered. You would be surprised how many companies suddenly need people at the last minute. Your letter could be lying on someone's desk, and you get offered a job!

■ Apply to work for a campsite operator. They often take younger people and although the work is hard, the atmosphere is great!

Job-changers, women returners, mature entrants

Anyone looking for a career change could search for prospective employers by looking through the Association of Independent Tour Operators (AITO) brochure (see Chapter 14) or on their Web site. Also try the *BITOA Handbook* (see Chapter 14 for the British Incoming Tour Operators Association). Companies included in these brochures offer a more individual service to clients, so are more likely to require staff with more mature knowledge.

TIP

Companies mentioned in these booklets are often very small, so it makes sense to phone first to ask about possible vacancies before you waste their time and yours. Generally companies aren't too worried about age, but will be interested if you have something to offer, such as knowledge of specialist subjects for which they offer holidays, or geographic knowledge of obscure places they might feature.

When applying for a job, comments like 'When I organised an expedition to the area you feature in your brochure...' or 'I see your company takes Americans on Jane Austen tours, and I lecture on her life' or 'My hobby is...' will get more attention than 'I had a wonderful holiday in...'.

Tour operators develop and produce their product and, as in all manufacturing industries, there are many different jobs that go to make up the end product.

Career progression

Many directors of tour operating companies started as overseas representatives and then moved into the head office when they had had enough of the sun, sand and working 24-hour days. Now they only work 12–15 hours a day!

TIP

After working for a large tour operator, many people see a niche for small, specialised tours, and leave to start up their own operation.

If you like flexible working hours and are adaptable enough to enjoy being involved with tour planning one day, and helping out with the new brochures the next, it is relatively easy to work your way up to the top in most companies.

IS A JOB WITH A SPECIALIST COMPANY FOR YOU?

- Do you have good communications skills?

- Are you good at selling?

- Do you speak another language?

- Do you have a Travel Geography qualification, History of Art, History or other useful degree?

- Do you have common sense?

- Are you prepared to dress smartly when working? When in charge of 40 VIPs you have to dress the part; in some countries you will have to wear a tie (for men) or tights (for women) whatever the temperature.

The smaller the company, the more adaptable you have to be. Working under pressure is part of most jobs, and you may need to discipline yourself to work in an orderly and methodical manner (difficult for the extroverts that often fit well into this industry). If you forget to book plane tickets you could have 40 angry customers and no job!

2

Travel agents

THE EMPLOYERS

A travel agent sells tour operators' holidays, accommodation, transport, etc, to the general public, and/or to selected companies arranging travel for their employees (this type of agent is generally known as an 'implant').

Travel agencies may be individually owned, be part of a chain, or in some cases be owned by a tour operator. Staff should be able to advise customers on best buys, suitable destinations and most convenient routes appropriate to their needs, as well as handling bookings and ticketing.

Most agencies will be members of ABTA; some will have an IATA licence to enable them to issue airline tickets. Theoretically anyone can open a travel agency, but most customers will look for the reassurance of ABTA membership before booking.

THE JOBS

Travel agency sales consultants, also known as travel agency sales clerks, advise clients and sell them holidays and travel. Much of their time is spent dealing with clients in person.

You talk to clients to find out what type of holiday they want – many clients are looking for package holidays. You would show them holiday brochures, answer any questions and may suggest particular resorts or hotels.

When clients have chosen a holiday, you check by computer to see what is available. If they accept, you book the holiday using a computer system linked to the tour operator. You collect a deposit from the clients, then fill in booking forms. You would collect the rest of the payment some weeks before the holiday. The tour operator sends the holiday tickets to the travel agency, which then passes them on to the clients.

You would also deal with independent travellers who do not wish to use package holidays, but want to choose how to travel and where to stay. You may help clients plan their journey by using travel timetables and then book their air, rail or ferry tickets and accommodation.

You might specialise in business travel, dealing with complicated itineraries that can often be changed several times before the clients leave.

You would also offer clients advice on passport, visa and vaccination requirements, plus other services such as holiday insurance, car hire, excursions, foreign currency and traveller's cheques, etc.

You would handle cash, cheques and credit cards and must account for all money received. You may put up window displays, and deal with banking and general paperwork. As a consultant you would usually have sales targets that you must reach.

What is ABTA?

The Association of British Travel Agents (ABTA) was formed to help protect the general public. To operate as an ABTA member, a travel agent must have a certain percentage of staff who have taken ABTA-approved training, so the public can be sure that the person who sells them their holiday or travel is knowledgeable. The agent also has to pay 'bond' money, a safeguard in case it should fall into financial difficulties; this protects the money paid by customers, and gives them confidence to book.

All ABTA members agree to comply with codes of conduct that have been drawn up by ABTA in conjunction with the Office of Fair Trading. ABTA regularly scrutinises the finances of its members, which have to contribute to a central fund to pay out to safeguard the industry's good name, if a member goes bankrupt.

What is IATA?

The International Air Transport Association is the world organisation of over 200 scheduled airlines from over 90 countries. Members cooperate with the International Civil Aviation Organisation; they often co-ordinate international tariffs and speak with one voice in their dealings with governments and other regulatory bodies. To be an IATA-appointed travel agency, both here and abroad, an agency's staff must have IATA qualifications.

General employment

Most employers are 'high street' travel agents (agencies based in shops in major shopping areas) that sell leisure travel, ie holidays.

You can't just walk in off the street and ask for a job – you will need to take approved courses such as those offered by the Travel Training

Company (TTC), etc. Generally you will need to be taken on by a local agency as a trainee; if you don't know such an agency, TTC may be able to put you in touch with a local agent with a vacancy.

IT skills are necessary. Most tour operators provide all information on their holidays to agencies via a computer screen. You check availability and make bookings direct with the tour operator, ferry company, airline, car hire company, hotel, etc on the computer screen and print out confirmation of bookings whilst clients are present. Some agencies have a foreign exchange section that sells foreign currency and traveller's cheques.

If you want to work in an agency abroad, you may need to obtain an IATA-approved qualification that is also useful for some agency work in the UK. Each IATA qualification is worth a certain number of points towards the total required if you want to open your own agency. Some colleges in the UK offer courses that are worth IATA points.

Small, specialised agencies need people who know their area of specialisation, and they are sometimes prepared to take on older, unqualified staff because of their experience. Contact the Campaign for Real Travel Agents (CARTA) for a list of member agencies.

Travel counsellors are often staff with travel experience who work independently for clients who want an expert personal service. Most counsellors start by working for a high street agency and then branch out on their own.

Many agencies supply a uniform for work, and to wear on familiarisation trips. You often have to work at weekends.

TIP

Don't expect this to be a glamorous job; the general leisure travel agent is part of the high street, along with all the other shops. Counter clerks just sell travel instead of shoes or clothes. The only difference is that clerks in travel agencies have to take more intensive training courses.

Tom and Jaynie

Tom and Jaynie work for an agency that is part of a large chain of travel agents. Today they are on their first familiarisation trip as guests of a tour operator, which is taking travel agency staff from their area to see the types of holiday they promote to clients. Product knowledge will make it easier to sell the operator's holidays. Travel is one of the few products where customers put down money to buy a product they may never have seen, and can't try before they buy. So it gives the customer more confidence if the agent can say, 'When I was there…'. With everything paid for, including a gala dinner, Tom and Jaynic are really looking forward to the trip.

With 20 other staff from different agencies on the plane, they soon start making new friends. At the first hotel there is a cup of coffee, and then it's off to tour the bedrooms (taking notes), checking children's facilities, the dining room, the leisure complex and swimming pools, and then it's back on the coach and off to the next hotel.

Two more hotels before lunch, and then they can sit down for a meal. They share their table with staff from the local ground handlers who quiz them on what their clients need and what type of holidays they book.

After lunch it's in to the fourth (or is it fifth?) hotel, and there are three more properties, including self-catering, to visit before they arrive back at their hotel. They have 30 minutes in which to change for the gala dinner hosted by the tour operators' area manager. They have to be up at 7 am the next day, so it is early-ish to bed, before the wake-up call.

Back at work, the rest of the agency staff have all been on these 'fam' trips (short for familiarisation), so there are no comments about skiving off. Tom and Jaynie feel they need a holiday to recover from the trip, but thanks to all the notes they took they are able to give a presentation to the rest of the staff, and answer questions they know will be asked by clients.

GETTING STARTED

Working in a travel agency is all about selling, so any retail selling experience is helpful. Managerial staff are often taken on if they have experience in accountancy, marketing and sales.

TIP

Don't confuse working in a travel agency with working as a representative. Travel agency clerks sell holidays, reps meet and look after clients during their holidays – and strangely, if you are good at working in an agency, you may hate being a rep, and vice versa.

Try it out

Go into your local travel agent when it is quiet, and ask if you can sit and watch on a busy Saturday to see how counter clerks sell holidays. Offer to make the coffee – and take in choccie biscuits or a cake! If you like what you see, when it is quiet ask a senior person what they suggest for your next step.

If you live in a rural area or town, there are probably several coach companies locally. These can often offer employment, particularly if you aren't able to take a training course – they need staff capable of office administration, to sell coach tours, etc.

Useful qualifications

GCSEs or equivalents in English, maths and geography, literacy, numeracy and IT skills. GNVQs are useful as an introduction, but these *must* include the Travel Geography unit; ABTAC (ABTA Travel Agents' Certificate), British Airways Fares and Ticketing and IATA qualifications.

IS THIS THE JOB FOR YOU?

If you:

- like geography;
- are computer literate;
- have a good command of English;
- are a good organiser;
- are patient (clients can take ages to make up their mind) – then go for it!

OTHER WORK

There are also business travel agents (see Chapter 9) and implants – branches of agencies that operate inside a company, just handling the work for that company. This is a smaller sector, but the top agents, usually members of the Guild of Business Travel Agents, have turnovers in the millions.

There are also companies that deal in direct-sell holidays, airline seats, etc by telephone, with no face-to-face contact with the public.

Other agencies

Home workers

Recently many telephone and online travel agencies have started up successfully, where consultants start and run a business working from home. Some of these agencies deal with clients over the phone, others come via the Internet (see Chapter 11).

Call centres

This was an expanding section, particularly for airline bookings. However, recently many companies have out-sourced this work to India, closing down their UK operations.

3

Holiday representatives

THE EMPLOYERS

Sun, sand, sea and Sangria – do these words make you want to do this work? Or is it the real words of service, standards, stamina and sleeplessness that catch your attention? You are there to help solve problems – if there weren't any problems you wouldn't have a job.

Working as a rep, also known as 'holiday executive' or 'holiday rep', is a good start in the industry, and many people progress up the career ladder from this job:

- Most work is in European resorts – and you go where you are sent.
- You live in the resort, and generally share a room with another rep (of the same sex).
- Husband and wife teams can find work for campsite operators.
- For some work in the UK you work from home.

Tour operators need reps to work in a range of roles, including:

- resort rep;
- transfer rep;
- kiddies or children's rep;
- organiser for special interest holidays;
- senior citizen programme rep;
- family holiday rep;
- campsite rep;
- entertainer;

■ activity and sports rep;

■ chalet staff.

NB. Although most of the big tour operators own travel agencies, the following information does *not* refer to working in a travel agency. The job is not the same, and it is unusual for staff to cross over from one to another.

THE JOBS

Holiday or resort representatives/holiday executives

Age 21–35, although older people are accepted for 'senior' programmes and on campsites.

This is the most popular job, and thousands of staff are needed for summer and winter seasons. Spain is the most popular destination, followed by Turkey and Greece. Although France and Italy are top destinations with Britons, reps in these countries are usually locals – although not always.

Selection is very tough, as companies have to be certain you will understand and abide by the EU Package Tour Directive, especially with regard to safety and hygiene.

You could be working for a family holiday tour operator, on adventure holidays, sports breaks, or spa breaks, on campsites, with 18–30 age groups, flotilla sailing, culture breaks, etc. It all depends on your interests.

TIP

It helps to speak a language, particularly Spanish, French, Italian or Greek. Don't speak any? Start taking lessons if you want to show you are serious about a job in this sector. It impresses interviewers.

UK representatives

Age generally 18–55 , sometimes 60+.

Reps mostly work for schools with foreign students and for companies that specialise in 'adult education' holidays such as EF, Saga, Elder Hostel, etc.

Winter work

This could be in one of the resorts that generally have more sunshine than in the UK: Canary Islands, Florida, Majorca or the Costa del Sol in Spain.

Winter sports

Those reps who like skiing and snowboarding will jump at the chance to work in a mountain resort, but if you are able to ski – be careful. To be a recognised ski guide in most mountain resorts you have to take a long course to be qualified, and quite rightly expect to earn a good salary once qualified.

If you want to work as a ski guide go to a recognised Alpine ski school, where training is tough. After all, you have people's lives in your hands.

TIP

Take a basic reps course *before* applying to a company. Thomson, part of the giant German TUI company, says 'We like people who have invested in themselves.' If accepted, you will have to take a company training course, but it is often heavily biased towards understanding company paperwork, etc and you miss out on the 'hints and tips'. One distance learning course (www.tourismtraining.biz) helps with job-hunting by supplying a list of over 500 companies.

Mike

Working as part of a resort team for a major tour operator, Mike's job puts him in contact with many different people: hotel owners and managers, coach company staff and drivers, restaurant managers and waiters, excursion and venue staff, etc. He has to liaise with doctors and hospital staff, the British Consul, medical repatriation company staff and the police. However, if there weren't any problems, Mike says he wouldn't have a job!

A large part of his day is spent outdoors, even in the hottest or coldest weather, going between hotels and apartments, tourist venues and the office, or waiting in draughty airports or stations. 'Every day is different, so this is no job for someone who likes routine with a 9 to 5 schedule. However difficult your day, you must be able to smile and be attentive when a client asks a question, even if you are supposedly off duty. Some days can be long and tiring, especially changeover days (when one group of clients finish their holiday and a new group arrive). You do your morning's work, if lucky have a short break in the afternoon, then work right through taking departing clients to the airport, waiting and picking up new arrivals in the early hours of the morning. If there are flight delays you can find yourself working a 36 hour day.' Generally Mike has one day off a week, but if there is a crisis this may not be possible.

Mike started working in Spain (as do 60 per cent of reps), but as fashions changed, opportunities opened, and he was delighted to be offered a winter season in Cuba – his company's newest resort – as he speaks Spanish.

Mike's duties include:

- meeting clients at the airport, port or railway station and taking them to the resort;

- organising a welcome meeting to tell clients about the resort or area, what there is to do locally, and to promote excursions;

- visiting accommodation daily and being available at specified times;

- talking to clients and giving out information;

- sorting out problems, including finding lost luggage and passports, visiting sick clients in hospital, helping clients who have been robbed;

- completing paperwork in the resort office, sending reports and basic accounts to head office;

- liasing with hoteliers, apartment, chalet and villa owners or campsite staff;

- liaising with suppliers such as coach companies, restaurants, tourism venues and attractions;

- organising and selling excursions;

- accompanying or taking charge of excursions that do not need a local guide, and giving a microphone commentary.

A large number of reps' gripes centre around the dreaded night-time arrival; so why don't tour operators fly clients out during daylight hours? Holidays sold in the UK are often cheaper than similar ones sold in Europe. One of the most expensive parts of a holiday is the flight to the resort. On the Continent many airports do not allow flights to take off or land during the night, as this disturbs people's sleep. So aircraft can only do two 'rotations' during the hours an airport is open for flights. (A 'rotation' is a round trip made by an aircraft from base to destination and back again.)

In the UK, many airports remain open at night, so a plane can do at least three rotations in 24 hours, bringing down the cost of flights. But people don't like flying at night, so these flights are often cheaper.

Keeping costs down, operators schedule flights to arrive in the resort during the night, and return flights also take off at night.

A day in the life of a senior rep

Terry, a senior rep, says although every day is different, sometimes each one produces its particular problems. Here's one day, picked at random.

Yesterday was my day off, and as all the other reps were fit I didn't have to 'help out', so managed to spend most of the day catching up on sleep. Today I feel fit and ready to face anything!

9 am – Breakfast in my first hotel. Needed to try out the food as there had been complaints – otherwise I would have stayed in my flat and eaten in peace! Whilst trying to eat, clients kept on coming up to talk and ask questions. Still, suppose not eating is good for the waistline!

Visited three apartment complexes then, at midday held a welcome meeting for clients who arrived yesterday. I am getting good at these, and manage to sell an excursion to almost everyone.

Some clients buy several excursions – bless them! At first I was embarrassed to stand up and talk in front of clients, but now the other rep and I know enough to run a good double act together, with a lot of laughs. This is important. The basic salary is very low, so we need to earn commission from sales. The team shares this, so if I do badly they won't be very pleased.

1.30 pm – Time to take the excursion money into the office. This is always a worry in case it is stolen. Grab a sandwich and take it into the office to do my paperwork. As senior rep, I have more than most and sometimes wonder if the extra salary compensates. A report on a flight delay has to be sent to London, details of all the excursions sold the previous week, and an update on a client who had a heart attack.

4 pm – It's my turn on 'sick duty', so take a goodies bag up to local hospital to check on a young kid who had a nasty fracture when he slipped on the harbour steps. His face lights up when I come in sight; he loves digging into the bag to find puzzles.

5 pm – Phew! It's hot! Wish our company would hire air-conditioned cars for us (some hope); instead we get mopeds. I have to wear a crash helmet, which makes me even hotter, but it is a dismissable offence to ride without it. Call in to the coach company on my way back to check up on coaches for the transfers tonight.

6.30 pm – Collect the list of passengers for evening transfers. Going home, they will have been out of their rooms since midday today, and by the time we pick them up at 11 pm they won't be in the happiest of moods.

Back to the flat for a quick shower and change of uniform – yet again! Wash dirty uniforms in bath and hang to dry. Luckily in this heat they dry in a couple of hours. We are never given enough outfits to keep on top of the washing, but putting on a clean uniform is one way of kidding yourself you aren't really tired. After finishing checking pick-ups and a last minute look at passenger lists, manage time for an hour's cat nap but don't know if I feel better – or worse – afterwards.

9 pm – No problems! So time for a good meal with other reps and drivers before we set off for the airport. Talk is good once we get off the subject of football, and we all have a good laugh.

11 pm – Arrive at apartment complex and find everyone ready to go. Funnily enough returning clients are almost always on time. Suppose they are frightened of missing the plane. Give announcements out in coach and:

- Check they have passports and tickets.

- Explain procedure at the airport: put luggage on trolley then follow me with trolley to check-in desk operated by the ground handler (the company at the airport that handles incoming and outgoing flights on behalf of our company).

- Thank them for travelling with my company, and remind them of other holidays and short breaks they might like to book with us.

- Tell them about airport shopping.

- Say airport shops airside don't usually accept coins, so how about giving them to the driver?

- Then I check my paperwork to see who has booked and paid for extra leg room on the aircraft, families who should be sitting together, anyone who is extra tall and should be given extra legroom, etc. I have already made a note of these on the arrival transfer, had phoned the airline the day before, but it is as well to check again. I will be at the head of the airport queue to help if there is any problem.

Fingers crossed as we arrive at the airport. Will there be a 'delay' sign against our flight details? Wonderful. It's our lucky day, and the flight is on time to arrive at 2.30 am.

Tell the drivers to catch a nap on the back seats of their coaches. By law drivers aren't supposed to work more than a certain amount of hours, but they can still get tired with erratic shifts.

2.45 am – Weary passengers stumble out of customs, and grab luggage trolleys we have been guarding for them. No one says thanks, but have to be careful someone doesn't bump into my ankles.

4 am – Last passengers finally loaded onto the coach, and off we go. Have checked that everyone has seen the drivers loading their luggage onto the coaches. This has to be done very scientifically as there can be as many as seven 'drops' (places to leave clients) where the luggage has to come out in the correct sequence. Everyone curses if they have to waste time to go back if a suitcase is missed.

Whilst Stefano, my driver, loads the luggage, everyone boards the coach and I check their names again against my list. Finally we are off, and there is an hour's drive before we arrive at the resort. When everyone seems wide awake I launch into my CRESTT speech: Currency, Roads, Excursions, Shopping, Transport and Telephones. Once this is done we are nearly at the resort; I alert people to our drop-off sequence, and remind them there is a welcome party at 11 am.

As everyone gets off they collect their luggage and follow me in to the reception area of their accommodation. Luckily each place is well prepared, and I am glad to be able to leave the parents with kids in good hands and go off to the next place.

7 am – Climb stairs up to flat. My flat mate is in, so we swap stories of the day we have had. Set alarm for 10.15 ready for the welcome meeting at 11 am, and fall asleep after an eventful, tiring but interesting 24 hours.

Transfer reps

Age 18+.

Some large operators have so many transfers they employ staff just to meet clients and transfer them to their accommodation.

Special interest holidays

In the UK, many operators take over universities or public schools during the holiday and offer short courses covering a multitude of interests, from angling to zoology. Reps have to be good at administration, and it helps if they understand some of the specialist subjects. Most jobs are in the UK, but there are some abroad, especially for painting, etc.

Senior citizen reps

Age 35+.

Work in the UK and abroad, winter and summer. Some companies send clients to hotels in Spain, Cyprus and the Canaries for 4–10 weeks, so you have to be able to keep people entertained several evenings a week – bridge is popular, as are bingo and ballroom dancing. It helps if you have a nursing qualification.

Campsite reps

Age 18–60+.

Some operators are happy to take husband and wife teams. Work is generally welcoming guests, organising excursions and barbecue evenings, and sorting out problems, from leaking tents to medical emergencies.

If you are strong and physically fit, there is work putting up and taking down tents at the beginning and end of the season, and doing maintenance on site.

Entertainers

Age 18+ – 60+.

Tour operators often make use of home-grown talent for the 'reps cabaret' and other evening entertainment. If you can play a musical instrument, sing or dance, look for adverts in *The Stage*.

Activity/sports reps

Age 18+ until you are too old to play.

Companies offering sports holidays are growing rapidly; they provide everything sporting from flotilla sailing, riding holidays and cycling, to golf and tennis packages. You must have the appropriate sports qualification. Two types of reps are required: to look after kids aged from 8 to 18 at sports camps; and to work with parents, families and older clients.

This is one of the fastest-growing sectors, and there seems to be no limit to the sports on offer: if someone wants to play or take part, there is a specialist operator who will arrange a holiday – and need reps to look after the clients.

TIP

Beware of any company that employs you without asking to see your sports qualification. Sadly, even though there have been some dreadful accidents, the law still has loopholes, and if the company doesn't check you have the right qualifications to supervise or teach a sport, would you really be happy working for them?

GETTING STARTED

- Take a reps course: contact the Travel Training Company or the Tourism Training Organisation (see Chapter 14).

- Phone or e-mail tour operators for their application forms and read them carefully.

- If at first you don't succeed – well, some companies have over 50,000 applicants a year for perhaps 500 jobs – just keep on trying.

- Start learning a foreign language – it improves your chances of being selected.

IS THIS THE JOB FOR YOU?

- Are you prepared to work 24 hours or more at a stretch and still come up smiling?

- Do you like helping people?

- Can you act sensibly in a crisis?

- Do you have common sense?

If the answer is 'yes', you will probably love the work.

4

Tourism and tourist offices

THE EMPLOYERS

National tourist offices (NTOs), regional tourist boards, local authorities, tourist information centres, marketing groups made up of local tourism venues (conference centres, museums, stately homes, etc) all need staff to work in promotion, marketing and administration.

National tourist offices

A national tourist office is a country's representative office abroad, whose purpose is to promote tourism to its country. It provides locals with information regarding their country, and actively works to promote and encourage visitors. As part of its work it will liaise with airlines, travel agents, hotels, stores and the media, organising events and handling promotional activities that deliver the message 'now is the time' to visit its country.

> *TIP*
>
> Tourist boards in the UK publicise job opportunities on www.antor-offices.org.

UK tourist boards

Tourism is the second-biggest industry in the UK, worth £76 billion a year.

> ## TIP
>
> You have to speak a language for many tourist board jobs. Currently the top most-wanted languages are (in no particular order): German, Spanish, French, Italian, Turkish, Arabic, Korean, Chinese (major dialects), Japanese, Russian, Polish and Hungarian.

THE JOBS

National tourist offices

A number of tourist offices employ a public relations officer who may or may not be from the country represented, who must speak the language fluently. A tourist office generally uses a local advertising agency; sometimes this has its own publications department. In a few cases there may even be a locally employed conference and/or business travel specialist.

In the UK the main job opportunities for local staff working for overseas tourist offices are in the secretarial or information departments. IT skills apart, there is no defined way of entry to work in a foreign tourist office, though obviously knowledge and connections with the country concerned give you an edge.

Tourist boards

Tourist boards are funded jointly by government and tourism companies. Most boards have departments dealing with some or all of the following:

- planning and research;
- sales and distribution (selling publications);
- press and media relations;
- advertising;
- marketing;
- finance and special projects;
- research and development;
- strategic planning;
- special facilities: promotions and events;

- external relations;
- IT and office services;
- information;
- government and other liaison.

TIP

VisitBritain is particularly enthusiastic about promoting jobs in the tourism industry, and publishes several helpful careers information sheets; see Chapter 14 for contact details.

Regional tourist boards

The UK is split into regions, each of which has its own regional tourist board: a division of the national tourist board. Work involves marketing that specific region with the aid of promotions, publicity, events – and sometimes conference services. Staff numbers are not large (you would be surprised how few people manage to make a big impact) and competition for vacancies, when they arrive, is stiff.

TIP

Many tourist boards say they prefer a marketing degree to a travel and tourism qualification. Marketing is vitally important; tourism knowledge comes with experience in the job.

Tourist information centres (TICs)

TICs are scattered throughout the UK, wherever there are numerous visitors. They range from small, centrally located kiosks or caravans (closed in the off-season), to permanent centres with several employees. TICs are where visitors and locals come to seek information on where to stay, where to eat, how to find a certain attraction, what there is to see, what's happening locally, etc.

The information office may produce its own written material for tourist guidance, but is more likely to act as a distributor, and often makes money by charging local attractions to 'rack' their brochures. This money will go towards funding the TIC, perhaps to keep it open for longer hours.

Staff are generally locals with a good knowledge of the immediate area. Most work is over the counter, although larger TICs will have administration staff who will publicise the area, liaise with tourist board members and show visiting tour operators, journalists, etc around on fam (familiarisation) trips.

Competition for jobs is fierce, and for most TICs you must speak a 'useable' foreign language; for instance, Japanese is very useful in Edinburgh, while Swedish is useful in Newcastle upon Tyne because ferries from Scandinavia dock there. Obviously customer care experience, and a bright and helpful personality are required.

Alan

Alan says no two days are the same in a TIC, but the most usual question visitors ask is 'Where are the toilets?' Although the work involves dealing with the public, there are boring things to do such a replenishing the racks with literature – which seems to walk out the doors on its own.

The leaflets are free, but there are local guidebooks to sell, theatre tickets and BABA – Book a Bed Ahead – for people travelling without reservations. Most people ask him 'Which is the best hotel?', but he is not allowed to give recommendations, and has to operate a strictly fair allocation system.

Funnily enough, many callers are locals, wanting information on what is happening in their area. Even though Alan thought he knew the area well, there is always something new to discover. Callers not only need to know what is available locally, but also ask about bordering regions, and even want information about anywhere in the UK. So VisitBritain runs fam trips for TIC staff. These are great fun: everyone stays in a good hotel and is taken around by coach for a guided tour of the area selected, and gets to know the faces behind the voices on the phone. They swap hilarious stories about questions: 'Am I still in Italy' from one bewildered old client; or 'Why did the Queen build Windsor Castle under the Heathrow flight path?'

Winter should be fairly quiet, but with tour operators and hotels selling inexpensive weekend breaks, TICs are often nearly as busy at this time as at the height of the season, and stocktaking, answering letters and administrative work still have to be done.

When Alan uses his tourist board's official accommodation guide to make BABA bookings, Marie, the accommodation officer, will have checked them out.

Marie

I am a friendly person, but have to turn up incognito at hotels, guest houses, B&Bs, farmhouse accommodation and self-catering to check them out and act like an 'average' guest. I don't want them to lay out the red carpet just for me. When I do a major check, perhaps when a hotel applies to belong, or if we have received too many complaints, I book in under another name – and although I have checked beforehand that they have my booking, I can't tell you the number of times a receptionist will say 'You are not in the computer.' My reply is 'I'm a bit big,' but they don't get the joke.

When I am shown to my room, I have to carry out an inspection, from checking the mattresses to testing how effective the lighting is – there must be a certain amount of light per room. I have to order a drink from the bar, have a meal, then after breakfast I announce myself and will go through the problems with the manager and try and sort them out. Sometimes I tell them that everything is fine – those are the best days, seeing their faces!

My job can be lonely: eating on my own, and lots of driving between calls, but it is lovely to meet up with some of my farmhouse owners. I have known many of them since they first started, worked with them to improve their properties, and become a friend to many. I am not supposed to accept gifts, but they don't consider new-laid eggs or fresh clotted cream a 'gift'!

HOW TO FIND WORK

There is no precise entry way. It is really a question of luck, and being persistent. If the tourist board doesn't have any vacancies (sometimes advertised on its Web site), think of your local authority – most have a tourism department – and ask your local TIC for any 'tourism' associations based in your area: perhaps the local conference hotels have banded together as a marketing consortium, and network like mad at local Tourism Society 'dos'.

Go to exhibitions such as the British Travel Trade Fair in Birmingham, CONFEX at Earls Court in London, Visit Scotland in Glasgow, etc. Being a member of the Tourism Society sometimes gets you in for free. Key in words such as 'Tourism Marketing Consortium UK' on Google, and you would be surprised at the interesting leads that come back.

TIP

Equip yourself with your best 'tool' – a business card. There are a number of services on the Internet that print cards for a minuscule price.

Marketing groups

There are numerous marketing groups where operators or attractions and venues have banded together to run joint promotions, such as UK tour operators that sell holidays to France and have banded together under the ABTOF (Association of British Tour Operators to France) banner. They publicise holidays to France, and are a one-stop-shop for journalists wanting information about holidaying there.

The same system works from promoting conference venues to just about anywhere in the world. A group bands together to promote itself, generally to add to promotion done on its behalf by a regional or national tourist board. All these marketing groups need admin staff with IT experience, and preferably languages.

Qualifications and training

Before signing up for a course, ask what work experience you will be given – particularly if it is a sandwich course (employers love these). Time and time again employers say 'work experience is vital', particularly as if you enjoy the experience you will often be offered a full-time job when you finish your course/degree. Employers often say it doesn't matter what degree or course – it's what you make of it.

If you are a second careerist or returning to work, you may not need to take a course: your experience will be welcomed, particularly with consulting firms that handle tourism marketing accounts.

IS THIS THE JOB FOR YOU?

■ Are you enthusiastic?

■ Do you dress smartly for work?

■ Are you able to write reports?

■ Can you think laterally when you need to come up with ideas for promotions?

■ Are you able to enthuse others with your ideas?

▓ Are you willing to carry out market research and evaluate promotions?

▓ Are you happy to leave home before dawn to set up your company's stand at a trade fair, then break down the stand once the fair is over, returning home at midnight or later?

If the answer is 'yes', then a job in the tourism-marketing sector could be very interesting for you.

Senior tourism figure Mike Bugsgang, of Bugsgang & Associates, one of the top tourism marketing/PR companies, says:

> With over 25 years in the business, I describe myself as a tourism marketing junkie. Tourism is a brilliant industry to be part of and offers real career opportunities, particularly for those who are prepared to put something back. Valued in billions, tourism is obviously a serious business but it is also about fun and enjoyment, and new entrants should not lose sight of keeping a balance in this respect.
>
> One of the most important things I recommend to people joining our industry is to invest time in attending seminars organised by various bodies such as the Tourism Society and the Chartered Institute of Marketing Travel Industry Group (CIMTIG). The industry background information and networking opportunities provided by these events are invaluable.

5

Guides and tour managers

THE EMPLOYERS

Employers are tour operators, coach operators, city, town or regional authorities, factories open to the public, historic houses, castles, cathedrals and important churches, conference and incentive conference organisers, government agencies, museums, galleries, hotels, national parks, cycling, walking, adventure and riding tour operators, student tour companies, guided tour companies, walking tour companies, specialised tour operators, distilleries, farms schools, industrial heritage centres, associations, vineyards, gardens, Women's Institutes and similar organisations, regional and local tourist boards, and any company or venue that needs someone to look after visitors and show them around.

There are over 3,000 coach companies in the UK alone offering tours from day or short-break trips up to one- or-two-week holidays. Once it was the coach driver who gave the commentary, but this is now against the law, and research has proved that tours with guides are the first to be booked.

THE JOBS

Registered guides

Registered guides take a training course and are examined by the local tourist board or government agency. Successful candidates' names are then published in an official list or given out to enquirers looking for guides. In some places only registered guides are allowed to guide in certain historic buildings or areas. In the UK these guides are often known as 'Blue Badges' from the colour of their official badge.

Site guides

Generally site guides work in open-air areas such as historic monuments.

In-house guides

They work in stately homes, factories, distilleries, farms, museums, historic houses, castles, cathedrals and important churches, galleries and other tourist venues needing their own guides. The jobs can be full or part time. Once these guides were often volunteers, but as the tourism industry becomes more professional, venues increasingly pay their guides.

Trail guides

Trail guides work in national parks and tour operators need guides who are energetic and able to accompany visitors walking, cycling or riding.

Walking tour guides

This is the fastest expanding sector, when guides take visitors around an area, village or town. With more cities banning coaches from their historic centres, getting out of the coach and walking is often the only way to see a venue. Also, local authorities that offer ad hoc guided tours to passing tourists as part of their official promotions only have the guides' fee to pay, not the coach as well. This work is particularly suitable for those who want to set up their own company.

NB. Many guides who accept this type of work are paid per head – if lots of people turn up, you are well paid; but if only one person turns up, and the tour has been advertised and you have been booked to guide it, you still have to do the hour or 90 minute tour, and it has to be good, even though you only earn a few pence.

Tour guide

These are tour leaders who take groups overnight for short breaks and longer tours, generally by coach, but it can be by train or even plane, looking after passengers from the morning departure to evening arrival at the hotel, giving commentaries, handling tour administration and being on call 24 hours a day to handle any problems. A tour manager is an experienced tour guide. A tour director is a very experienced tour guide, speaking several languages, with in-depth knowledge of the history, geography, culture, food and economy of the countries visited on the tour.

There is work for those who want to start on their own, particularly as walking tour or specialised guides. See Chapter 11 on working from home.

Interpreters

This covers two types of work – first, those who 'interpret' the work or life of stately homes, industrial heritage sites, castles, mines, etc. You may be required to wear costume, particularly if the site recreates some period of history. People who have worked in industry are often welcomed for their specialised knowledge.

Other interpreting work is when you speak a language fluently and look after a specialised group, perhaps doctors or farmers, and give guided talks on the local scene on your way to appointments.

Guides tend to work in a town, city or specific area for a half or full day, and return home at night. Tour managers generally move around from place to place with their tourists, staying in hotels at night.

Most work is freelance, as guides are generally only hired to work when visitors arrive at a venue or go on tour. Interpreters may work for a different company every day, and even sometimes one company in the morning and another in the afternoon.

TIP

This is not the job for you if you like a regular working day; there will be some days when you work 12–15 hours, then there may be weeks with no work at all during the 'off' season.

Ian

Ian wanted to become a guide, but found the local tourist board only ran courses every other year – and this was the wrong year! So he took a distance learning course. The helpline recommended he contact a famous hotel nearby – make an appointment to see the hall porter. He did, and the hall porter said they often had overseas visitors who wanted to buy antiques. So Ian devised a walking tour, meeting guests at the hotel, walking them around the main sites and finishing up in an antique shop – where Ian arranged with the owner that he would introduce the clients, then pop into the back and make coffee for his visitors, who loved this welcoming touch. Ian worked out he would charge £50 for however many people wanted the tour (which lasted about 90 minutes) and he split the fee with the hall porter (who had the job of selling Ian's tour).

He printed up leaflets on his PC, which the porter distributed, and took some to the local information centre. If he got a booking from them, he paid them 10 per cent commission. But the real money-spinner was once Ian had become friendly with his guests: they loved his manner and knowledge, and he would offer to accompany them around the next day in their hired car (most had come this way). For this he charged £120 for the day, and gave the hall porter £20. He also received tips – not always, but enough to be a good bonus.

He spoke to an insurance broker, explained that he would be travelling as a passenger, and would need third-party cover in case he was sued by a client.

Ian then added more strings to his bow: the hotel had a conference department, so he went to see the banqueting manager and suggested three different tours he could take, aimed at up-market delegates and their partners. For these he charged a fee of £250 a day, which included organising lunch in a stately home, at extra cost. This only took a few minutes, once he had met up with the owner and arranged what type of menus were suitable, etc.

He is now taking the regional tourist board guide training course, and enjoying it more because he can relate the lectures to what he knows his clients want. It gives him an insight into more venues and ideas for his conference delegates, and places to take people in their cars. He is getting quite a reputation in the whole area for his tours – he has been on regional TV and had calls from three other hotels nearby wanting the same service. It took him about 18 months to get going, but now he makes a very reasonable living – from tourists in the summer, and conference delegates during the off-season.

TIPS

It is possible to 'mix and match' between local guiding work and touring, and this is the sensible thing to do if you need to work almost full time.

It takes time to build up contacts with employers, so you have to be able to support yourself when you start. Anyone who needs a full-time job might look for work at attractions that are open year-round.

Although 80 per cent of the world's tourism is 'handled' in English, if you speak a relevant language fluently it is easier to find work.

As a tour manager, once you have worked for one or two seasons with British groups, think of belonging to IATM (International Association of Tour Managers), take their certificate, and work with American and Asian groups, where pay is better.

For this work, you have to research and research. Make friends with your local library and don't rely on the Internet, where information might be unreliable.

Valerie

Valerie started out taking groups on overnight coach trips to Italy. She thought there must be better jobs available, so went into a very smart restaurant with coaches in its car park, asked the manageress which companies she could recommend, and ended up with a name and telephone number to contact. They offered her a job taking Americans around Europe, following the route she had taken with the overnight trips, staying in hotels and in much more comfort.

She realised there was more to the job than she thought, so in between tours she haunted the local library, taking notes on everything from flora and fauna to geography and the current economy of the countries they visited. On tour she would point her passengers in the direction of the night life, then retire to her room to read up for the next day's commentary.

This paid off, and she was offered more and more interesting and well-paid tours. She now works exclusively for two companies, and takes her pick of their best tours. As Italy is her favourite country, she makes sure that as many tours as possible go there, although she has taken tours to over 40 different countries.

Looking after an arts group, she took them to a special Fabergé exhibition. Talking to the curator, she asked him if he had ever considered organising an exhibition to display the incredible craftsmanship of the Huguenots who had been exiled from France – Fabergé came from one of these families, and other Huguenots made their mark working in silver and architecture, even founding the Bank of England. The Curator paid her the compliment of saying this was the first question he had been asked that day that made him think! It made Valerie think too, and she is now thinking of setting up her own tours, 'On the Huguenot Trail'.

GETTING STARTED

You need maturity for this work, so generally people come into this sector when they are 25 or over, although some tour managers start out looking after 'cheap and cheerful' British coach tours when they are aged 20+. Almost any job can lead to guiding, from gardening to cooking, as so many groups now want to be accompanied by an expert. Teachers often become tour guides, as do actors – both professions have an affinity with guiding.

Teachers have to be careful not to be too 'teacher like'; you are not talking to a class, but leading adults who have paid good money to be looked after, not lectured. Actors need to be aware that if you accept a guiding job, you *cannot* cancel it if an audition turns up; once you do this you get a name for being unreliable, and work dries up. You also need to remember that visitors have come to see the country, not you. I once asked a Turkish guide why he guided standing up in the coach (which is illegal); 'So people can see me' was the reply. He wasn't very popular, and the company soon sacked him.

A good training course will help with finding a job; you cannot expect the tourist board that runs a course to provide work, but you can expect them to hire lecturers who work in the industry, and give you tips about finding work.

TIP

Be prepared to phone, phone and phone again to find work. Most companies that employ guides and tour managers are small, and may only need one or two staff each year. So you have to spread your net wide and be persistent.

6

Chalets and villas

THE EMPLOYERS

Staying in a chalet on a winter sports holiday is almost entirely a UK phenomenon. Pioneers such as Sir Arnold Lunn 'discovered' winter sports at the beginning of the 20th century. After World War II, British holidaymakers, subject to strict monetary exchange controls, couldn't take enough money out of the UK to pay for hotels, so they developed the 'chalet' concept as a way of making their precious allowance go further.

At first ski enthusiasts used to hire a chalet themselves, invite friends to stay, and hope they paid enough to cover expenses. Gradually, as more people went into this market, standards improved, and today over 1 million Britons go abroad for winter sports, many of them staying in chalets.

Holidaymakers who enjoyed this type of holiday were targeted by companies operating summer villa holidays, and now this concept gives consumers a vast choice, from simple Greek tavernas to luxury five star villas with their own swimming pool and top chefs hired to cook for guests.

Penny

During her Cordon Bleu cookery course, Penny heard about a chalet company looking for cooks. They owned a massive chalet (really a small hotel) and needed an extra hand in the kitchen as someone had fallen in the snow and broken their ankle.

Penny loved skiing and was hoping for the chance to hit the slopes, but realised she would be on trial and have to work very hard. Luckily she got on well with James, the head chef, who liked the tiny strips she cut when asked to 'julienne' some vegetables. Gradually Penny got into the swing of the job. She was up very early each morning to prepare a full English breakfast for the guests. Afterwards it was on with preparing that evening's dinner, then, the bit Penny liked most, making the cakes which every guest helped themselves to when they returned off the slopes at the end of the afternoon.

One guest left behind a rather cheap bottle of whisky instead of a tip – so Penny suggested using it to make her mother's whisky cake. This was a such a success that it is now a feature of the company's advertised menus. Once the cakes were made, Penny and the others were able to grab a couple of hours on the slopes; everyone working for the company received a free ski pass, which was a big help.

Then it was back to the evening shift, and the day ended around 10 pm. Penny did so well that at the end of the season the company offered her a summer job, but this time as head cook in a smaller villa, with an assistant to help.

THE JOBS

Esprit are one of leaders in this sector, and say they look for the following.

Chalet chef

- Cooking quality meals.
- Guiding and training chalet assistants.
- Budgeting and menu planning.
- Preparing and serving meals to Esprit standards.
- Ensuring that your chalet is hygienic and safe for your guests to stay in and for you to work in.
- Stock management.
- Daily cleaning of all kitchen areas and equipment.

Requirements:

- Qualified chef or a very experienced cook.
- Good communication and interpersonal skills are essential.
- Age 21 years plus.

Chalet cook

▧ Responsible for guest care and routine in a small chalet.

▧ Providing guests with information on services, the resort and activities.

▧ Providing a welcoming and safe environment, building a rapport with guests and dealing with problems.

▧ Cooking quality meals to Esprit's standards and dietary requirements.

▧ Budgeting, menu planning and stock control.

▧ Ensuring high standards of hygiene and safety.

▧ Daily cleaning of kitchen and communal areas, and twice-weekly complete chalet clean.

Requirements:

▧ Socially outgoing, dedicated and enthusiastic.

▧ Cooking qualifications or experience are essential.

▧ Age 21 years plus.

Chalet representatives

▧ Assisting the chalet chef with the running of a chalet.

▧ Providing guests with information on services, the resort and activities.

▧ Providing a welcoming and safe environment, building a rapport with guests and dealing with problems.

▧ Assisting with stock taking, receipt of deliveries, food preparation and other kitchen duties.

▧ Ensuring your chalet is hygienic and safe for your guests to stay in and for you to work in.

▧ Daily cleaning of kitchen and communal areas, and twice-weekly complete chalet clean.

▧ Hosting guests on arrival and during evening meals.

Requirements:

▧ Cooking qualifications are not needed, but hospitality experience an advantage.

▧ Age 21 years plus.

Maintenance buildings officers (MBOs)

MBOs are prepared to use their muscles gathering up all the rubbish, sweeping the steps and pathways clear of snow, driving guests up to the ski lifts, and generally humping stores around. In summer you clean out the pool, drive guests to ferries/beaches, etc. To find such a job, you can look on company Web sites, ask friends, or just turn up in a resort and ask around.

TIP

You don't have to ski to do this job – it is just a perk – and accommodation is very basic in the chalet (usually next to the underground store).

TRAINING AND QUALIFICATIONS

Any good catering qualification is suitable. Some staff will do a full chef's course, while others take special chalet staff short courses at well-known cooking schools.

On the water

7

CRUISING

Cruising is one of the fastest-growing sectors in the tourism industry, with bigger and more luxurious liners being launched to satisfy demand. Once a pastime for the rich and famous, cruising slumped during the oil crisis of the 1970s, but is now staging a come back. Passengers appreciate not having to pack and unpack every time they move on, and to a certain extent they feel they are cocooned against terrorism – and cruise liners, on the whole, have good security. Although cost does affect the traveller, it is the high level of customer service on board that attracts new and repeat business.

Working on a cruise ship is probably the most exciting way to travel and see the world, and the industry offers year-round employment. Miami is now the cruise capital of the world, poised facing the Caribbean with good weather year-round.

Working environment

Your working environment is dependent on your job on board. The higher up the career ladder, the more glamorous conditions will be. Below deck, where passenger contact is limited or even non-existent, working and living conditions can be cramped, with long hours. You will probably have to share a tiny cabin, with no porthole, with one or more crew members.

If your role involves customer service, you will have a more varied day and free time; sometimes with privileges such as using various services on board that are normally reserved for passengers.

> ## TIP
>
> Sea-sickness affects travellers whether they are workers or passengers. The doctor on board can normally assist and you will find your sea legs after a couple of days. Nelson suffered from seasickness all his life.

The jobs

Ashore, the admin offices of cruise lines rely heavily on large marketing and sales departments, reservations, press and PR. On board, admin includes office duties.

On the operational side on board, the main jobs are for bar staff, stewards and chefs. Entertainers are in constant demand and, of course, ships have medical and engineering teams. Large cruise liners require hairdressers, fitness and sports instructors, sales people for their shops and boutiques and croupiers when they have a casino on board.

Steward/stewardess

Stewards and stewardesses on the catering side serve in restaurants or work in the pantry or stores. On the cabin side, they make beds and clean cabins. Promotion is generally from within, so a waiter could move on to be a section waiter, to an assistant head waiter, and then to head waiter. Alternatively, promotion might lead to public room barman or bar services manager.

Cruise lines will provide accommodation and food but in some cases you may be expected to pay or contribute to the cost of your uniform. The usual minimum age for recruitment is 20. Many shipping companies now use recruitment agencies for staff, such as Logbridge or those that advertise in trade magazines.

> ## TIP
>
> Stewards/stewardesses and pursers may have to work seven days a week with little free time, and hairdressers and sales staff (unlike officers, entertainers and social hostesses) do not mix with the passengers.

Purser

The purser is the head of 'hotel services afloat' and directly responsible to the captain. It is a job that requires excellent organisational skills and diplomacy, patience, courtesy and tact. The pursers' bureau answers questions, cashes traveller's cheques and deals with all the documentation and the crew work of the ship. So accounting and clerical skills are essential.

Initial recruitment is as a junior assistant purser. Qualifications are good secretarial skills and a minimum of two years' experience, reception and cash handling experience. Knowledge of a continental language is a definitive advantage. Many companies regard the new Air Cabin Crew Vocational Qualification as a good foundation course (both air and cruise crew need similar customer care skills).

Here's the experience of Pat, who has been working on one the of world's largest liners for six months.

Pat

Basically my work is secretarial, but each time I go outside the office I see a different scene – from whales swimming alongside to bustling ports in the Caribbean. Beats the daily commute any time! We work long hours, but are given time off at the end of a series of cruises, and one day off a week.

7.30 am – Early start today selling last-minute shore excursions; even before I have a chance of slipping into the office there is a queue of passengers waiting to book. More and more we try and encourage people to book all their excursions at the beginning of the cruise (even offering a discount), but there are always people who can't make up their minds – except at the last minute!

Life is fun, but there are little niggles, like the passengers who say, 'I would love a job like yours – seeing all those fascinating ports.' Yes, from the gangway entrance – but as soon as we have checked everyone onto the coaches for the start of a shore excursion, it's back to the office.

Once the passengers are all off for the day, we get down to the paperwork, from ordering the massive amount of food that is needed to feed everyone, to liaising with the head chef to ensure that the right supplies come on at the right port.

Coffee with the head chef, who collects unusual coffee recipes, and when in port gives all us coffee addicts a treat. Today it is some special Columbian beans, and I easily find my way to his office by the aroma.

Down to lunch in the staff canteen – not as glamorous as the passengers' dining rooms, but we are well fed.

Today is the day for the monthly delivery of drinking glasses – you wouldn't believe how many are broken each voyage. Our glass manufacturer in England has a major logistical problem sending out 20,000 glasses a month to meet up with us at ports of call. I check that they have been delivered, count the number of cases, and talk to the storeman to ensure that if any are missing or broken, he will let me know.

Just time to slip ashore and do some shopping. I am beginning to know my way around and have favourite shoe stores, a wonderful bookshop where I love to browse, and today I will be stocking up on perfume for presents as the prices are rock bottom here.

Back on board to hear the passengers enjoyed their day out – well, one or two didn't, but amongst the hundreds we carry, that's not a bad average. Then it's down to the cabin I share with the other purser's secretary to change for the crew Karaoke night.

Hotel manager

Major cruise liners are so large that passengers can imagine they are on land – and the ship is run exactly like a hotel. There will be a hotel manager, with the same responsibilities as one on shore, aided by housekeeping staff. As a career move, hotel staff often work a year or two on board, to gain experience.

Medical staff

Most liners will carry a doctor, with a back-up team to carry out minor surgery. Registered General Nurses are required, particularly those with specialised training.

'Dialysis cruises'

In 1980 Dr Rittich from Hamburg organised the first 'dialysis cruise' for patients on kidney dialysis. Demand was so great that now kidney dialysis is offered on liners around the world, with clients returning year after year.

Fresenius operates machines on cruise liners such as MS Deutschland. According to 'dialysis holiday' expert Christine Gledhill of Freedom Apartments and Hotels, this is one of the most popular liners with UK passengers, cruising the world, from the Arctic to Asia, stopping off in the Mediterranean, South Seas and other exotic places. There are eight stations in its dialysis unit, so if you have renal nursing qualifications this could be a full-time job.

Health, fitness and beauty

Today it is no longer enough to offer passengers different ports of call. Whilst on board they want to be pampered, or work on their fitness regime. Cruise ships have extremely well-equipped gyms or fitness rooms, with every new machine you could think of. There is work available for those with a fitness, sport or aerobics qualification.

Hairdressing or beauty treatment qualifications mean you may be offered a job right away without having to wait for a vacancy.

Retail

Most passengers come from a higher income bracket than the usual package holidaymaker; cruise ships eager to cater for these high-spending clients want sales staff with good retail experience.

Other jobs

Qualified infant or junior school teachers, or anyone with NNEB qualifications are needed as children's hostesses.

Printers, photographers, telephonists and cinema projectionists are also wanted in the pursers' department.

Recruitment

There is tremendous competition for jobs and once accepted, there can be a wait of up to two years before a berth (place) becomes available. Miami is now the cruise capital of the world, and the majority of jobs will be for ships out of this port. Cruises are far shorter than those out of other countries (the majority last from four to seven days, so it means that it is easier for staff to leave) and provide openings for more crew. Cruise companies recruit via agencies in the UK.

TIP

If interviewed and selected in the UK, it is usually a requirement, particularly if you join your ship in Miami, that you buy a return air ticket. This ensures the expense doesn't fall on the company if you decide cruising is not for you and want to come home.

Celebrity Cruises and Disney make regular visits to London to recruit staff, looking for a minimum of two years' experience in hotel or restaurant work. Two useful Web sites are: www.shipjobs.com and www.crewbar.net.

Cruise ship training

Most positions are transferred from a shore job where the jobholders already have the necessary qualifications, eg secretaries and hotel managers. However, a new one-year Vocational Qualification for Air Cabin Crew is proving popular for cruise and ferry work; the two are very similar. Information is available from Pan Aviation Services on 020 7371 8731, panaviation@yahoo.com.

Everybody can improve his or her chances of obtaining a job through attending a customer service course. Ask the local tourist board for details of the 'Welcome Host' day courses.

FERRIES

Many people still prefer to travel by car, and ferries are reporting increasing business. The loss of 'duty free' allowances affected some services, but there have been innovative marketing ideas to encourage customers, especially cheaper travel off-peak.

There are ferry ports around the UK: Belfast, Dover, Fishguard, Hull, Portsmouth, Stranraer, Holyhead, Southampton, the Scottish coast, Newcastle upon Tyne, Harwich, etc, where staff working for the various companies are based. Although many staff live on board for their shift, unless they work on one of the big North Sea ferries they will probably vacate their cabin for their opposite number on the next shift, so they need to be based locally.

Staff include stewards/stewardesses, pursers, catering staff, retail staff for the 'duty free shops', deckhands, engineers and officers. Most employment is seasonal; full-time employment may be offered if the operation is year-round.

Working on ferries can help with obtaining employment on cruise ships: if you show you can work well, and understand what is needed, this looks good when going for an interview. For most positions you must be 18 or over, able to work shifts (this could be 24 hours on, 24 hours off) and to work in a team.

Languages are useful: French, Dutch and German for the English Channel routes; Scandinavian languages for those across the North Sea; and Spanish and Portuguese for the routes to northern Spain.

Hoverspeed operates seasonal services on the Dover–Calais and Newhaven–Dieppe routes. It looks for on-board deck crew for its high-speed Seacat catamarans, to help load and unload all vehicle traffic and assist with all aspects of safety and cleanliness on the car deck.

Candidates should hold either an Efficient Deck Hand or AB (Able-bodied Seaman) certificate, have good communication skills, demonstrate confidence in dealing with the travelling public, and remain calm under pressure. Crews work shift patterns that include weekend and bank holiday working, and are based in Dover or Newhaven.

Currently pay for cabin crew/customer services staff on ferries is up to £8 per hour including shift allowances and bonuses.

In Scotland, Caledonian MacBrayne operates numerous ferries between the mainland and islands. Its support services are based in Gourock, where departments include HR, marketing, public affairs, safety, purchasing, information services, operations, technical, catering, reservations and finance. Relevant qualifications would be required for each of these departments. Clerical staff and pier staff are also employed at outport offices, located throughout the west of Scotland.

Deck crew and port staff generally need First Aid, personal survival techniques and fire prevention qualifications. See the Maritime and Coastguard Agency Web site, www.mcga.gov.uk, under Seafarer Standards for details of training courses.

If you want to work abroad but go home at night, some companies recruit UK-based staff for their sites in Calais and Boulogne.

Employers

Some major employers are:

- www.Brittany-Ferries.com;

- www.calmac.co.uk (Caledonian MacBrayne);

- www.hoverspeed.com;

- www.Norfolkline.com;

- www.seafrance.com;

- www.stenaline.co.uk.

Training

For sales training, the Passenger Shipping Agency (PSA) is the trade association representing most companies, and it organises officially approved courses for travel agency staff to help increase sales, including:

- Essentials and Dynamics of Cruising: an overview of the cruise industry.

- Managing Cruise Sales: a course covering time management, market planning and media relations.

- Don't Tell – Sell: designed for call centre supervisors and staff in junior management.

Those who are not members of the PSA's Retail Scheme are charged £56.00 plus VAT per day course.

FLOTILLA AND OTHER SAILING HOLIDAYS

Abroad, many companies offer yacht charters around the world for bareboat sailing (the hirer does the work onboard!) and for skippered and fully crewed charters (crew included). There are numerous jobs working on these yachts; skills required are sailing competence (courses are organised by the Royal Yachting Association) or, for cabin and catering crew, similar skills to those needed for chalet and villa staff.

For those who don't want to hire or own a private yacht, flotilla sailing provides plenty of adventure without having to be an expert. Companies like Mark Warner (www.markwarner.co.uk) look for staff to work in the Mediterranean and Caribbean.

Jobs

Waterfront managers manage staff, equipment and financial organisation for the 'waterside' element of a resort holiday. In charge of the instructors, they devise a daily rota for staff. Generally 22+, with RYA/BWSF instructor qualifications in at least two water sports, SBDA/RYA Powerboat level 2 competence and First Aid.

Instructors (sailing, windsurfing, water-skiing), 19+ with BWSF/RYA qualifications, RYA Powerboat level 2 for windsurfing and water-ski instruction and First Aid.

OTHER JOBS

There are jobs on canal barges and narrow boats, sailing ships, private yachts, motorboats, etc around the world.

Customers love the relaxing aspect of UK boating holidays, exploring the countryside from the canal or riverside at around 3 mph, passing stunning landscapes that cannot be seen from the road. Similar holidays are offered by UK operators along the vast network of European canals, particularly France.

Employers

Hoseasons is probably the largest company in this field, but as it acts as an agent for individual boat owners or small companies, you would need to contact these for work; possible jobs could be for mechanics and engineers for servicing. Hoseasons itself employs 250 staff at its call centre in Lowestoft, selling holidays at parks and lodges, as well as boats. Check out the following:

- www.blakes.co.uk;
- www.hoseasons.co.uk;
- www.cruisefrance.com;
- www.bargecompany.com;
- www.vfbholidays.co.uk.

Abroad, many canals are wider, carrying larger hotel boats with a skipper and crew, which often includes a guide to organise excursions and sightseeing tours. Rivers, particularly the Rhine and the Danube, carry massive hotel ships operated by companies such as Peter Deilman and KD.

8

Conservation and eco-tourism

Today, the majority of tour operators are concerned about conserving the planet, realising the concrete developments of the last century were counterproductive.

Where once this chapter would have highlighted good practices, today these are part and parcel of most tourism programmes. Increasingly conservation forms part of a package tour, and it is AITO's stated policy to raise the level of environmental awareness. Its members are at the forefront of conservation practices, carrying out environmental audits as a matter of course.

Nowadays the average tourist is aware of the harm tourism can do to the local environment, and books holidays with conservation built in. The type of holiday in which the visitor takes part in local life, albeit only for a short time, is expanding. Boutique hotels, where a group of old houses has been converted sympathetically to offer discrete luxury, are the most popular places to stay. Even business clients are forsaking the high-rise international chain hotel for these eco-friendly hotels.

Adventure holidays, particularly those visiting far-flung venues, are increasingly popular, but tourists are much more likely to avoid the well-trodden route, and take time to learn about an area. For example, Everest has become a bit of a mess, with large numbers of climbers leaving their rubbish behind; today's savvy traveller is more likely to be involved in a project to clean up the route, and in doing so get to meet locals who welcome their presence.

Sporting holidays offering specialist activities such as surfing are becoming increasingly popular. Cornwall, and in particular the beaches at Newquay, are inundated with people who go there to ride the waves, and provide much-needed employment in the area.

Overall, eco-awareness has moved on from the 1970s and 1980s, when countries such as Turkey nearly ruined their ecology by allowing massive concrete development. Today, explorer and conservationist David Bellamy frequently says that tourism is going to be the saviour of many conservation projects.

David Bellamy

David Bellamy admits that properly managed tours are necessary for conservation. 'Their mere presence, as well as their money', is good for animal welfare. According to him, there would be no game left in the Tsavo National Park if it weren't for tourists. Similar reserves only survive because governments now understand tourists will pay more to see game alive than it is worth to the locals dead. Bellamy believes 'the only hope now for so many of the world's animal species is tourism'.

There is a need for conservation officers around the world to help preserve our ecology; 'sometimes it's just a matter of teaching locals how to tie up a boat' on a reef, without ruining the coral – simple, but Bellamy believes this is the way forward.

THE EMPLOYERS

These include national and country parks, heritage sites, wildlife conservation areas, farms, hotels, tour operators, destination management companies, cruise lines, airlines, conference centres, national and regional tourist associations, and conference and visitor bureaux.

Jim Selman

Sunvil Holidays are keen to protect the environment of places where it takes clients, and appointed Jim Selman to develop good environmental practices at its resorts. Jim's job involved the local mayors and dignitaries, working together to preserve the best features and encourage traditional crafts, architecture, food, etc.

Jim is developing ecologically friendly holidays for Sunvil clients, such as walking and cycling tours – so eventually they will need reps who like walking, know how mend a puncture, etc.

The National Trust

The National Trust, the largest landowner in the UK after the government, owns properties, parks, farms and even villages that need a range of staff, from stewards and trail guides to wardens.

The National Trust expects its staff to 'show an appreciation of its aims and objectives'. It needs land agents for estate management, which includes care of historic buildings, environmental protection and nature conservation; archaeologists, wardens and foresters whose work involves implementation of practical conservation work; architects, building managers and clerks of works, carpenters and masons experienced in traditional methods; specialist advisers on the conservation of textiles, paper, stone, paintings, pottery and ceramics, and international environmental monitoring.

Then there are administrators and property managers, housekeeping staff and those involved in marketing, PR and fund-raising, and more – from running a holiday cottage booking service to supporting local crafts when buying goods for National Trust shops. In fact, a mini-army of staff. For more information send an sae for 'Working with the National Trust'; see Chapter 14.

The Landmark Trust is a similar organisation, devoted to preserving buildings and letting them out to sympathetic visitors. It often works in conjunction with the National Trust; for example, the National Trust owns Lundy Island, and the Landmark Trust lets out the cottages on the island. All these properties will need administration staff in lettings departments.

Heritage sites

English Heritage is the largest employer in this sector, but there are other private and local authority-owned sites around the UK needing staff: custodians, architects, etc.

Wildlife conservation areas, including parks and nature reserves

In this sector, opportunities arise in unexpected places. For example, the Falkland Islands now have an Environmental Planning Officer, whose job is crucial to the holiday plans of increasing numbers of visitors to one of the last largely unspoiled places on earth. Duties include monitoring the oil exploration currently taking place; you will find similar jobs around many coastlines.

Farms

Regional tourist boards have special officers whose job is to liaise with the farming community and develop tourism in an environmentally sympathetic fashion. Farming is vitally important to tourism: when visitors think of the UK, they see fields with cows and sheep grazing in them – no farms means no fields, hedges, walls and animals for tourists to photograph.

THE JOBS

Jobs in this sector are often allied to other disciplines – architecture, nature studies, etc, and large organisations may have only one or two vacancies a year, especially as many are charities. It is worth contacting the following and asking if they can point you in the right direction: Crafts Council (020 7278 7700): Countryside Commission (01242 521381); Forestry Commission (0131 334 0303); Department of National Heritage (020 7211 6267); and English Heritage (020 7973 3000).

TIP

We haven't mentioned many of the organisations concerned with conservation, as they are charities and do not have a large staff to answer questions. Key 'conservation' into a search engine, and see how many organisations come up! If you ask for literature, it is a nice gesture to send a small donation.

National and country parks

These need wardens, rangers, admin staff, trail guides, etc. Conservation is built into each job specification, and their operations are dedicated to preserving and conserving flora, wildlife, etc.

Hotels, tour operators, airlines, cruise lines, tourist and conference bureaux

Many have a dedicated member of staff who carries out environmental audits. Regional tourist boards, the Tourism Society, The Royal Geographical Society, etc often run conferences on tourism and the environment, and a look at delegates' lists gives you ideas of companies to approach for jobs.

Adventure and exploration tours

Normally, you have to be aged 23+, with good First Aid skills. Sometimes a PCV (passenger carrying vehicle) or LGV (large goods vehicle) licence is required. Then the sky is your limit, with jobs on offer around the world. One of the best ways to get ideas of potential employers is to look up www.aito.co.uk, and trawl through the different specialists tours offered by member companies.

Green Globe is a worldwide environmental management and awareness programme for the travel and tourist industry, open to companies committed to improvements in environmental practice. Look for information of companies to approach on its Web site (see Chapter 14).

GETTING STARTED

Studying agriculture, architecture, horticulture, forestry, etc all provide a good background for work in this sector. Often conservation jobs happen because someone has an interest in the subject, has a chance conversation with someone else, and gets a job offer – so get networking! It really works.

The European Incentive and Business Travel Meetings Exhibition (www.eibtm.ch) is very keen on environmental initiatives, and the UK Institute for Conservation (www.ukic.org.uk) publishes useful background leaflets dealing with conservation.

Qualifications and training

For information on NVQs in environmental subjects, contact the British Trust for Conservation Volunteers, or in Northern Ireland, Conservation Volunteers NI. Both organisations run practical training weeks, where you learn conservation techniques while doing a navvy's work – and you have to pay for this! But you do learn how to use chain saws, and other gizmos. Contact www.btcv.org, Tel: 01491–821600, or www.cvni.org, Tel: 028 9064 5169.

IS THIS THE JOB FOR YOU?

▓ Are you diplomatic?

▓ Could you mediate in a 'triangle' of problems reconciling the interests of visitors, community and countryside?

▓ Are you concerned about the environment?

> **TIP**
>
> Many people now working in this field started by reading all they could about conservation and ecological matters. If you understand the issues, you can often find work experience in this field, which eventually leads to a career.

9

Business travel

THE EMPLOYERS

VisitBritain say roughly one-third of UK tourism income comes from business travel: people visiting for meetings, conferences, exhibitions and the like.

People handling this sector work for travel agents, implants (clerks or consultants working for a travel agency inside a major client's office), conference organisers, incentive travel companies, car hire, etc.

THE JOBS

Business travel arrangements are made for anyone visiting a destination in a business capacity as opposed to going on holiday. Hence an airline's 'business class' is geared to frequent business travellers who need that extra amount of leg room to work on their laptop. Hence also the 'business' hotel, which offers services such as 24-hour room service, mini-bars, same-day valet service, a business centre, Internet access in rooms, etc.

Business travel may involve individuals or a group. Work in this sector may mean making travel arrangements for one person, or several company executives attending a conference.

Most UK business travel companies will belong to the Guild of Business Travel Agents, each of whose turnover can be £20–50 million a year, yet are generally unknown outside their sector because they don't deal with the general public.

Conferences

Planning, organising and running conferences is a large part of business travel, and a huge employment area. However, most PCOs (professional conference organisers) are small firms, and it can be difficult to find your way in. Networking is helpful; contact ACE (Association for Conferences and Events; see Chapter 14) and take out student membership so you can attend their functions, exhibitions, etc.

Professional conference organiser

PCO 'pitch' to an association, organisation, firm, etc. to run their conference. Once approved, they do some or all of the following: select the venue, send out information to delegates, handle bookings, organise speakers, negotiate rates with venues and hotels, restaurants, coach companies, etc, organise and handle finance, register delegates, ensure the conference runs smoothly, and send out 'thank you letters' after it is all over.

Their work starts months or even years ahead for some major conferences. Sometimes work involves organising an exhibition to run alongside a conference, or the conference is part of an exhibition.

Conference hotels/venues/towns

Most major hotels have a conference and banqueting department; many towns have conference bureaux and want to promote their town as the ideal conference destination. Sadly, London's flagship conference venue, the QEII hall, only takes 990 people, when many towns abroad regularly host events for 4,000–5,000 people, increasing their tourism yield. However, places such as Birmingham, Edinburgh, Brighton, etc have thriving centres, hosting many international events.

A conference officer working for a conference bureau is 'selling' the venues in the town or area, so has to have an in-depth knowledge of each venue, the services offered, size and capacity, and available dates. Hence marketing qualifications are useful.

In-house conference organisation

Many firms think organising a conference is easy, and ask their staff to do this. Next year they either call in a PCO, or decide to do the thing properly and start up a special department – it is not as easy as it looks!

Incentive travel

Incentive trips are rewards companies offer their personnel for increased business, hard work, etc. Sales teams are often the target – those selling over and above certain amounts are eligible for an award. Studies prove travel is the best incentive or motivator, but it must be a trip people couldn't buy for themselves.

There are growing numbers of travel companies specialising in incentive travel arrangements. A recent survey showed 30 companies with turnovers in the millions – up to £47 million per year. These companies put together various holiday elements to provide a luxury package going somewhere unusual and/or exotic, where staff take part in something they couldn't do by themselves. You have to be imaginative and creative: theme parties, unusual venues and out-of-the-ordinary events become the norm. The only limit is your imagination – and expertise to organise whatever programme has been chosen.

Business travel clerk

This job needs someone with an excellent knowledge of geography. When a client asks for a 'flight to Tirana tomorrow' you have to know where it is (Albania) the best way to get there (Austrian Airlines via Vienna), what visas and jabs are needed, and which is the best hotel.

You may never meet a client face-to-face, as most contacts are by telephone or e-mail. The work itself can be highly pressurised, with companies' representatives and individuals needing carefully tailored itineraries worked out to a strict timetable. One client may need a straightforward flight booking, while another may be making several flights and train journeys, needing enough times for connections, plus hotel bookings, hire cars, etc over a period of weeks. Even a single flight booking can involve a choice of 50 different prices, routes and times, which you have to sort out to come up with the deal best suited to the company's travel policy. And then, when you have everything worked out and booked – your client comes through and says it's all cancelled and now they are going three days later. You grit your teeth, and get on with re-booking.

Most of the work is done within the travel agent's offices, using e-mail, phone, fax and the post to receive instructions, make bookings, print tickets, etc, which are then taken by courier to the client. Paperwork tends to be relegated to the end of the day as the phone and e-mail take precedence and dictate the work pace.

Pay rates tend to be higher than for those selling holiday travel, because of the more complex nature of the work and the extra knowledge required.

Corporate hospitality

This is when a company invites favoured clients or suppliers for a day out, choosing somewhere special such as Derby Day, rugby finals or polo, or perhaps arranging a private event at a stately home with balloon ascents, go-karting, falconry, etc.

Catering has to be of the highest standard, as does safety, so there are job opportunities here, especially for anyone who likes hard work in a different venue almost every day.

Polo

Polo has a very glitzy image, making it ideal as an up-market day out to entertain clients. It is a typically British sport (we introduced it to the rest of the world when we discovered it in India), and is played at gorgeous country venues, often on private grounds.

The final of the British Open Polo Championship for the Veuve Clicquot Gold Cup represents world-class sporting action. Polo is exclusive; it is played on such a huge ground (up to nine times the size of a football pitch) that it doesn't come over well on TV, but when guests are there to watch the action, they find it thrilling.

Cowdray Park in Sussex is *the* Polo club in the UK, and now produces corporate hospitality packages that include champagne reception, superb luncheon with fine wines, afternoon tea, VIP grandstand seats, reserved car parking and souvenir programme. Firms buy a package, and often ask someone to give an introductory talk in their private marquee to explain what is meant by 'riding off', and why a sandwich isn't a good thing. Guests return year after year.

TIP

There are over 50 polo clubs around the UK, plus clay pigeon shooting clubs, falconry displays at stately homes (Scone Palace is one) and other places used for corporate hospitality. It is worthwhile phoning to see if there are any such days planned and who the organisers are – then phone them to see if there is any work going. Once you are in, you should be able to make lots of contacts to help with more work.

GETTING STARTED

It is highly unlikely you will find a job advert for incentive and conference executives; jobs come because someone knows someone – so networking is important, at ACE, Tourism Society 'dos', etc. Although NVQs are being developed, the basics for getting a job are IT skills, hard work and being there at the right time.

Qualifications and training

Travel geography is useful; any charity work, particularly running events, is extremely important for your CV.

There are courses offered by colleges, but it is worth finding out which textbooks are used and to make sure that it is tailored to European work practice. The good news is that experience is highly regarded, so this is the ideal job for women returners, second careerists, etc.

TIP

If you really want to do this work, ask local conference venues for names of organisers who are booked to run a conference there. Then phone them and ask if they have any temporary work for a local. It will take time. You may only get one day's work at a time (if you are lucky), but it is one of the surest ways in.

If you are lucky enough to get a day's work, turn up early and dress smartly – a suit in a sober colour, plus tie, tights (as appropriate) and anything your Mum approves of.

Then start phoning organisers again – but this time you have a day's experience, and it is surprising what you can learn in 10 hours.

IS THIS THE JOB FOR YOU?

- Do you like geography and map reading?
- Can you think on your feet and produce accurate work?
- Do you like researching?
- Can you change out of 'setting up' clothes into smart gear in 5 minutes?
- Are you happy working all hours?

Yes? Then business travel needs you!

10

PR, press and promotions work

THE EMPLOYERS

Employers include major tour operators, destinations marketing bureaux, national tourist offices, major tourist attractions, airlines, tourist boards, public relations companies.

THE JOBS

You may work in-house for a tour company, or for a PR company handling tourism accounts. Your job will be to produce as much favourable publicity as possible for your company or client, help promote the company to clients, and if there is a crisis, handle this effectively so that you have the media on your side, rather than looking for an unhelpful story.

TIP

The worst scenario for an airline is a crash, such as the one British Midland suffered at Kegworth. But the way it was handled produced admiration from the media.

Within the hour the CEO, Sir Michael Bishop, was on TV to express condolences, etc. No excuses, no hiding behind 'our official spokesman'; the buck stopped on his desk. He made it very clear his first priority was to find out what had happened, and help relatives and survivors in any way he and his company could.

Creativity or a flow of ideas is important, particularly when working with a limited budget. Knowledge of print, layout and production costs is often helpful. Many journalists transfer over to this sector, and a course in marketing or communications is helpful.

Sarah

Sarah works as a travel account director in a public relations firm. Now in her late 20s, she left school to take a two-year bilingual secretarial course, and 'the language really helped; when I'd completed the course I went off to Paris and was immediately offered a job as a temp with an ad agency (not hard to find if you go to agencies situated in the agency district). When I returned to England I knew enough about how the industry worked to feel confident in approaching one of the largest agencies, and this time was taken on as a copywriter'.

Her experience and language helped her become an assistant account executive, where running the account on a day-to-day level, liaising constantly with the client, coordinating press trips, organising events and press conferences, and burning the midnight oil thinking up ideas for promotions, gave her a fascinating job. Before she knew it, her fluent French meant promotion, travelling every few days on Eurostar to Paris visiting the French arm of her agency's biggest client. Now she is an account director, she finds she has to keep a tight rein on budgets. She has been asked to take on two other clients with an office in Paris, so she is now in charge of three accounts.

Travel writer

This is everyone's dream job – except that the reality is rather mundane. Because it is considered a 'glamour' job, writers can be told they won't get paid, 'because you are getting a free holiday'. A good travel writer is not on holiday – he or she is in a resort or area to find out as much as possible that will interest readers. Work starts after an early breakfast and can go on until midnight.

Competition for jobs is fierce, and often work is offered to someone already on the staff. One of the best routes in is the secretarial route – you may be offered 'free' weekends, provided you write a travel article on your return: your newspaper gets seven days work a week out of you. Grit your teeth; eventually persistence pays – or at least you hope so.

Otherwise, apply to a local newspaper as an indentured trainee – if you can find one that will take you on. Slog around the courts and flower shows, and take a course accredited by the National Council for the Training of Journalists (see Chapter 14). The same advice applies to travel photographers.

Events management

This is a much more secure field! Events include exhibitions, promotions, pop concerts, open air shows, agricultural shows, and almost anywhere where people gather to attend a function. There is work for organisers, sales staff to sell exhibition stand space, promoting and advertising events, designers, and often freelance work during an event for receptionists, stewarding, interpreters, stand staff, demonstrators, etc.

Many exhibitions are held abroad; if a company is exhibiting, it may well design and ship its stand abroad, taking along carpenters, builders, electricians, handymen and drivers.

For jobs you would apply to the company actually organising the event – the venue will be able to tell you who it is.

QUALIFICATIONS AND TRAINING

All media courses will teach you the theory of travel writing and photography. If you don't want to be left jobless at the end of the course, make sure you ask searching questions about work experience, because that is what will get you a job.

IT skills are important in most jobs, and languages can be very, very useful.

IS THIS THE JOB FOR YOU?

- Are you thick-skinned?
- Can you accept criticism of your work?
- Are you tenacious?
- Do you have a retentive memory for facts and useful information?
- Do you have stamina?
- Do you will realise you will have to constantly check, check and check again? Whether it's the Chairman's car, or the technician who is going to be available in case anyone's PowerPoint presentation doesn't work – if something goes wrong, you are at fault, even if it was nothing to do with you.

If you are happy with your answers to these questions, you will survive! Good luck.

11

Working from home

WHAT TYPE OF WORK?

Probably a third of tourism companies operate from home – with offices ranging from the kitchen table to purpose-built outbuildings.

Many well-known tourism companies started this way. Until you have tested the market you don't know if your idea is going to work. However much market research you carry out, the tourism industry is dealing in dreams, and people can be unpredictable.

Talk to an accountant or Business Link about potential tax and Council Tax implications. Generally speaking most local authorities are relaxed about working from home – it keeps traffic off the streets if nothing else!

To work successfully from home, you must have a suitable area – the kitchen table is fine as long as it doesn't need to be cleared every time someone wants a meal. You also need to be disciplined and settle down to a working day in your home – although you are going to be around for your kids, children need constant attention (particularly if you are there), so you may need to make arrangements for someone to take them off your hands for a period every day.

TIPS

Loneliness is seldom a problem. You have to get out to check venues, meet clients, attend exhibitions, etc, so you avoid one of the biggest problems of home working.

Another tip: get a dog! Many homeworkers get so absorbed they go on far too long staring at their PC – a dog has to be exercised, which makes you take a break.

Betty

Betty thought working from home meant she could look after the twins. However, she soon found that it didn't make for a professional approach. They sensed when she was absorbed in a business conversation, and would demand attention.

So she found a neighbour who had been a child-minder; the twins spend four hours a day with her, enabling Betty to get on with concentrated work. Once they return, Betty does jobs like answering her e-mail, which she can leave if the twins need attention.

Having to complete the major portion of her work within four hours 'concentrates my mind wonderfully', and if she has to go off on fam trips the twins stay with her neighbour.

Betty's job involves finding families where businessmen and women can stay whilst studying English at language schools. She has a contract to supply suitable accommodation for stays of 2 to 10 weeks. The homes have to be similar to the 'students' homes; en-suite bathrooms, high-quality beds and furnishings, and large rooms with a desk.

Guests pay between £60 and £100 per night, Betty taking 15 per cent. Hosts provide the room, make the beds and clean, provide breakfast, five dinners a week and Sunday lunch.

Guests are treated as part of the family, so it is important Betty ensures they have something in common with their hosts. One important aspect is to make sure that the family has a proper dinner around the table five times a week (the other two nights guests are expected to take themselves to the local pub or restaurant). Guests are there to learn English, and family conversation is one of the best teachers.

She thought she might have trouble in finding suitable places, but word of mouth soon produced over 50 properties, ranging from rooms with a senior professor at the local university to a couple of stately homes.

There aren't too many problems – she had to move one guest who hadn't told her he hated children, and she had placed him with a delightful family who had six! Otherwise, the guests usually end up best of friends, returning for holidays with their host family.

THE JOBS

Tourism is a service industry, but some services would not be cost-effective if supplied by a big company with large overheads. However, a home-based company might be able to fill a niche and make a profit. Companies based at home include:

- meet-and-greet services at ports and airports;
- brochure design;
- coach brokering;
- e-bookings;
- hotel and airline booking agents;
- corporate hospitality;
- conference organisation;
- student home-stays;
- specialist tours, eg ex-forces personnel interested in history taking small groups of visitors to battlefields.

Judy

Judy loved her job as a registered guide, but became frustrated at the way visitors were all shoved on 'milk run' tours – they were easy for the company to set up, but she felt tours should be tailored to clients' needs, not company convenience. While at a tourist board event, she met a conference organiser who told Judy she was looking for fresh ideas for something for partners to do during conferences.

Judy sent her some ideas, and three months later (when she had forgotten their conversation) the organiser came back to book her for two day tours. These were a great success – and the organiser booked her for more.

Judy then went back to the conference hotel, saw the banqueting manager, and suggested he might like to offer other organisers similar tours. The manager saw this as a marketing opportunity, encouraging companies to book his hotel rather than a rival.

Now Judy belongs to ACE (Association for Conferences and Events). 'I get about half my business from contacts I meet at their events'. She also has a good relationship with three hotels in her area, offering different tours to each hotel, so no one is jealous.

IS THIS THE JOB FOR YOU?

▨ Are you prepared to join associations, tourist boards, etc? There is an enormous support system from the Tourism Society, Business Link (0845 600 9006), Regional Tourist Boards, local Chambers of Commerce and local tourism marketing groups.

▨ With up to 30 per cent of people now doing some or all of their work from home, do you know any local businesses that work from home? If so, ask for advice.

▨ Do you have a good accountant? Unless you are trained, the best advice anyone offers is get an accountant – they will save you more than they cost.

12

Further career opportunities

Travel and tourism covers a wide range of career opportunities. In addition to those described earlier, this chapter briefly outlines further areas of opportunity.

Employers

Many employers are holiday centres, theme parks, etc such as Butlins, Disney, Center Parcs, Alton Towers, Thorpe Park etc – the list is endless. Throwing the old 'holiday camp' ethos out the window, these companies offer a very high-quality 'holiday experience' for guests. Generally this is a totally-inclusive programme with activities, events and entertainment.

These companies must market, sell and promote themselves, and will have a huge division working on this side. Staff who come face-to-face with customers include Disney 'cast members' who walk around in cartoon character outfits, catering staff, sports instructors, children's nursing staff, entertainers, etc.

Health clubs

Health is such a topical subject that it has turned into a profitable industry in its own right. Many hotels now offer a club or spa, with 'designer' pools and beauty therapists providing the latest treatments. Many of these clubs and spas are operated as a franchise from a large company, so you would be working for them rather than the hotel. There is work for receptionists, fitness experts and therapists.

Stately homes

These can belong to a massive organisation such as the National Trust, or be individually owned such as members of the Historic Houses

Association. Upkeep costs are high, so property owners have to think of ways to pay for repairs, etc. To do this they organise events: weddings, upmarket B&B overnight guests, letting the building and grounds out for corporate hospitality events, and of course opening to the public.

Most properties will need staff in their a tea-room (a big money spinner); they market and sell guide books; sometimes they offer guided tours at an extra cost, etc. They need staff to manage and keep up the property, as well as an efficient promotions and marketing team – sometimes just one person!

Bed and breakfast

This traditional British industry has now been updated. Many frequent travellers find they want a change from hotel accommodation; it is a little known fact that if you are looking for somewhere to stay, particularly in places like London, companies are now setting up reservations systems so that people can book to stay in private homes. These homes offer en-suite bathrooms with their bedrooms, and often the guests have sole use of a sitting and/or dining room.

Farm tourism

The countryside has always been a magnet for visitors, and the foot-and-mouth crisis accelerated many farmers' decision to go into B&B, self-catering, etc. Now many who offer these services say they make more money from this side of their business than from traditional farming.

Coach companies

With over 6,000 coach companies in the UK, there are job opportunities for drivers, engineers, operations and administrative staff, freelance guides and tour managers. On the continent there are thousands more coach companies, particularly in Germany, France, Italy, Belgium, the Netherlands and Spain. These often employ British coach drivers and tour managers, provided they speak the appropriate language, in carrying American and Asian clients.

Many coach companies operate their own excursions and tour programmes, in the UK and on the continent.

The coach tour market

Graham Beacom, Chief Executive of the Coach Tourism Council, says the traditional market for coach tours in the UK, the 55 plus age group, is expanding. They have better health, are wealthier and more discerning, and last year took 8.8 million domestic coach holiday trips, and 2.2 million coach trips overseas.

The UK's coach tourism industry now reflects the travel industry overall – with short breaks, city breaks, centred holidays, two-centred holidays and the coach tour itself. Members are using more upmarket vehicles – one company now offers 'grand touring' coach tours with more leg room: passengers are prepared to pay a 12 per cent premium for this facility.

Other factors keeping the coach market buoyant are a fear of flying, and the power of VisitBritain. This organisation has recently diverted funds from promoting the UK abroad to promoting it to the British – and its campaign is paying off.

Courses

The Chartered Institute of Transport can advise on courses for the Certificate of Professional Competence for Coach Company Traffic Managers.

Most regional tourist boards arrange courses for their members, or you could ask the Tourism Training Organisation's helpline for advice on suitable training (see Chapter 14).

TIP

There are thousands of 'unknown' jobs in travel; one way to learn about some of the many opportunities is to visit travel trade exhibitions. Normally these are by invitation, or cost £10 to £20 entrance fee. If you belong to a trade organization such as your local tourist board or the Tourism Society, you are alerted when these exhibitions take place, and usually get free entrance.

Railways

Eurostar

Train staff, platform staff and administration work for Eurostar (www.eurostar.com). All staff (train and catering) go through a rigorous safety training. Eurostar's onboard catering crew are employees of Momentum Services Ltd.

Eurostar

When Eurostar first started it recruited many staff from airlines. Cabin crew liked being able to return home at night and not suffer jet lag – and wages compared favourably with airline pay. However, Eurostar experienced problems with airline crew, 'as often they don't speak French fluently'. So now its recruitment is more focused, targeting people with fluency in French and, if possible Dutch, German, Italian, Spanish or Asian languages – those spoken by their passengers.

If you work for Eurostar there may be opportunities to transfer to, or work with European railways such as SNCF (French railways) and SNCB (Belgian railways).

Other railways

Across the world, trains are becoming more luxurious. Australia has opened up its line right across the Continent, and will soon offer trips. Spain has taken great leaps forward, as have Germany and Italy (for long distance trains – the less said about some local trains the better).

In Switzerland the trains run so precisely that the ticket office will print you out a complicated itinerary telling you times, which platform and even what type of refreshments are available on each sector. As someone said, 'Swiss trains are just like having your own personal taxi, particularly as you wheel your luggage straight to the platform at Geneva or Zurich, and often the station is right opposite the hotel.' Their trains even have shops on board – with opportunities for travelling retail staff.

Leisure and hospitality

The employers

The leisure and hospitality sectors feed off tourism, and both are booming. Theme parks, heritage centres, sports and leisure centres, national and wildlife parks, special events, etc report increased business, as do hotels, restaurants and pubs.

Airlines, particularly budget operations, are now flying throughout the year, and usually show load factors in the high 80s or 90 per cent. People now look for a cheap fare for a weekend break, then use hotels, restaurants, attractions, shops, etc, bringing income in 12 months a year.

The jobs

You can start at any time, from 16 to 60, and this sector is full of gap-year and holiday jobs. Try out a different sector each holiday: theme parks often look for temporary staff, as do historic houses, country parks and gardens, theatres, heritage centres, sport and leisure centres, zoos and wildlife parks.

TIP

If you like your temporary job, speak to the personnel officer for advice about qualifications and where to get training.

Qualifications and training

You may be advised to go abroad; Switzerland is noted for hotel schools, as is Cornell University in the USA. Contact the Sports Council, Countryside Commission, Institute of Leisure and Amenity Management, Pan-Aviation Training Services, etc; see Chapters 13 and 14.

Are these jobs for you?

▓ Do you like dealing with people?

▓ Are you passionate about food, service, welcoming guests?

▓ Are you fond of animals?

▓ Do you enjoy sports?

Did you answer 'yes' to one or more questions? Go for it!

Luxury holidays

Luxury holidays are on the increase and taken by clients prepared to pay for exclusive services. Nothing surprises travel agents who handle this type of booking; if someone has the money, they can arrange the holiday – however unusual or exotic – whether it be a weekend break to South Africa, a stay at an exclusive spa hotel or the newest special interest holiday. All they have to ensure is that the holiday is the best available, with first-class airline travel, luxury hotels and special additions such as balloon rides, chauffeur-driven cars and hotels with individual butlers for the best rooms. Languages are particularly useful for work in this sector.

13

Training and qualifications

Travel and tourism is one of the most popular subjects offered at colleges. There are many qualifications from which to choose, ranging from GCSEs, GNVQs, the new VCE (Vocational Certificate of Education), HNDs and Degrees, up to an MBA. However, there is no overall industry lead body, and it is up to individual employers to decide which qualifications they require. At the time of publication the Government is looking into qualifications, but so far there is no definite guide, neither is there is an overall 'travel and tourism' qualification.

Before signing up for a course, we strongly advise you to:

- Ask the personnel departments of potential employers' companies what qualifications they require.

- Ask for contact details of ex-students who have taken the course, and find out if they have jobs in the industry.

- Check: will the course rely on paper projects, or do you have genuine work experience? If so, is this relevant to the type of work you want to do?

- Check: what are teachers' links with employers? Have they worked in the industry? (If the college brushes you off, this could be an indication of the quality (or otherwise) of the course.)

Many companies ask for such specific skills that they may prefer you to have a good general degree, such as marketing, and add industry knowledge once you are working.

Courses

This is an outline of some of the courses available.

Age 16+: GCSE, GNVQ and VCE

These qualifications can be taken at schools or colleges, and form a basic foundation for many jobs in travel and tourism. The following assessment boards can supply a list of courses; it is up to you to check if the courses are suitable for the type of work you want to do:

- City and Guilds, 1 Giltspur Street, London EC1A 9DD, Tel: 020 7294 2800, Web site: www.city-and-guilds.co.uk

- Edexcel, 32 Russell Square, London WC1B 5DY, Tel: 0870 240 9800, Web site: www.edexcel.org.uk

- OCR, 1 Regent Street, Cambridge CB2 1GG, Tel: 01223 552552, Web site: www.ocr.org.uk

NB. Some colleges offer courses in British Airways or IATA Fares and Ticketing. These courses are suitable if you want to work for a travel agency, or a company handling air tickets, but not necessary for representatives and many other jobs in tourism.

Age 16–24: Travel agency/tour operator

Contact TTC (Travel Training Company) for details of training and qualifications for travel agency and tour operations. If you are eligible, there may be a suitable Modern Apprenticeship available. You will need four GCSEs at Grade C or above, or a GNVQ in Leisure and Tourism. Trainees work in an agency or company and undertake training leading to the Travel Services NVQ Levels 2 and 3. Amongst the courses on offer are:

- ABTA Travel Agents Certificate (ABTAC) in Travel (Travel Agency) is the standard qualification for travel agents. Participants study by registering with one of TTC's partner colleges.

- ABTA Tour Operators Certificate (ABTOC). Now known as the Certificate in Travel (tour operators), this is the qualification for tour operators.

- Administration N/SVQ qualifications.

- Air Fares and Ticketing Course approved by IATA in the UK, available at Foundation, Primary and Advanced levels in TTC partner colleges. Before signing up, make sure this is the right qualification for the work you want to do.

- Call Centre Qualifications. These cover Call Handling Operations, Supervisory Call Handling and Managing Call Handling. Scottish/National Vocational Qualifications.

- Modern Apprenticeships are being phased out. Ask TTC for details of replacement qualifications.

Holiday representatives

Suitable short courses include First Aid, a basic hygiene course, distance learning courses, relevant sports qualifications such as BASI (British Association of Snowsports Instructors) and NVQs in customer care. Some colleges offer holiday rep training, but ensure teachers have actually worked as reps. The Tourism Training Organisation has a helpline giving advice and details of distance learning courses; see Chapter 14.

Children's representatives

Most companies will ask for NNEB or an N/SVQ in childcare, or a CCE (Childcare and Education Certificate). Many local authorities run suitable training courses. Ask at your town hall, or contact CACHE (see Chapter 14). www.Kids-Holiday-Reps.co.uk also runs courses.

Cabin crew

There is a Vocational Qualification (for airlines and cruise/ferries) devised by Pat Egan of Pan-Aviation Services, now offered in over 14 colleges. KLM and other airlines employ students.

Chalet/villa staff

These staff will need City & Guilds or Catering NVQs, or Diplomas provided on private cookery courses, which often offer courses designed for chalet staff.

VisitBritain offers Diplomas covering basic food hygiene, 'Welcome Host' training, basic health and safety at work and a certificate in regional tourism knowledge.

A food hygiene certificate is useful for rep, chalet and villa work. Your local education authority will have details of suitable courses; the four-day environmental health course is suitable for reps, etc.

A First Aid course is always useful. St Johns Ambulance, the Red Cross and sometimes a local general hospital run courses, and will teach you how to look after children that are injured. In the USA many local hospitals run 'baby-sitting' courses, so if you are there on a long holiday it is worthwhile checking these out.

S/NVQs

To find out more about travel and tourism S/NVQ routes into work, contact TTENTO; see Chapter 14.

Languages

If you speak a language you are more employable. All business languages are useful. Currently VisitBritain is spending £6 million on a marketing campaign targeting 'new' markets including Poland, Russia, China and South Korea. Consider taking a language as an option with any course, and taking part of the course abroad. Ask CILT (Centre for Information on Language Teaching) for advice; see Chapter 14.

HNDs, degrees and MBAs

UCAS (Universities & Colleges Admissions Service) currently lists over 1,250 tourism and 142 travel courses available. Below is a list of the types of companies that may employ you and some of the courses that might be suitable (contact UCAS for details; see Chapter 14):

■ *Employer:* Adventure and expedition tour operation. *Possible course titles:* Adventure tourism, Adventure tourism management, Leisure tourism, Sport tourism, Sport tourism management.

■ *Employer:* Attractions and theme parks. *Possible course titles:* Tourism attractions management, Tourism development studies.

■ *Employer:* Eco-tourism. *Possible course titles:* Ecotourism, European tourism, Global tourism, Rural tourism, Sustainable tourism, Tourism resource management.

■ *Employer:* Cultural tourism. *Possible course titles:* Cultural tourism, Heritage tourism.

■ *Employer:* General management and administration. *Possible course titles:* International tourism, International tourism management, Tourism business management, Tourism management, Tourism management studies, Tourism operational management.

■ *Employer:* Marketing. *Possible courses:* Tourism marketing. Many employers such as tourist boards are very happy with a good management degree. Sales or marketing courses/degrees are highly thought of by most tourist boards, tour operators, etc, which say a degree in these subjects is often more useful than a tourism qualification. CIMTIG (Chartered Institute Marketing Travel Industry Group) can offer advice on suitable marketing courses; see Chapter 14.

■ *Employer:* Travel agencies/tour operators. See Travel Training Company details below.

■ *Employer:* E-commerce. Surrey University has developed a course on e-commerce for the travel industry.

Over 25, women returners, career changers, mature entrants

Consider what you can offer an individual travel agent or specialised tour operator. Contact CARTA, Advantage or AITO for a list of members where your previous experience may be useful. Be prepared to take 'top up' courses, short courses, etc. The Institute of Marketing (CIMTIG section) offers suitable courses.

Additional courses

Art and design qualifications are useful when working in brochure design and production. Bookkeeping up to a degree in finance is also useful, especially if you eventually want to run your own company.

Working abroad

The EU says that nationals of one EU country who want to work in another EU country have to have an internationally recognised qualification (75/368 Directive on Mutual Recognition of Qualifications). Most courses recommended here offer suitable qualifications.

Funding your studies

There are Career Development Loans that can sometimes help you with money for a course and also cover some living expenses; see Chapter 14 for contact details.

Mentoring

Still unsure of what qualification? The Tourism Society offers members a mentoring scheme for women, which they believe could have a positive impact on their careers. They are organising a combination of 'one-to-one mentoring' with a mentoring coordinator matching the needs of the mentees with the expertise of the mentors, and a series of women-oriented initiatives such as workshops and networking events.

NB. There is *no* positive discrimination! The scheme will be open to both male and female mentors.

After qualification

Many employers now use psychometric tests to screen job applicants. Regardless of how good your qualifications might be you may still be asked to do a short verbal numerical reasoning test as part of the entry procedure. For more information on this and a selection of practice tests, turn to the Appendix at the end of this book.

14

Useful addresses and further reading

Today, associations and companies are downsizing, getting rid of those nice helpful staff who answered questions. Instead, they encourage you to go on their Web site, or send an e-mail in which you fill in various fields (which can be time-consuming) so that they get the information in a form that is quicker to read. If you don't have access to the Internet, most local libraries have PCs you can use and staff will help you if you can't master computers. In the list of useful addresses below, phone numbers have been included where associations welcome telephone enquiries.

USEFUL ADDRESSES

ABTA (Association of British Travel Agents)
Newman Street, London W1T 3AH, Tel: 0901 201 5050 68, Web site: www.abta.com. Has an interesting vacancies page.

ACE (Association for Conferences and Events)
Riverside House, High Street, Huntingdon PE29 3SG, Tel: 01480 457 595, Web site: www.martex.co.uk/ACE

Advantage (National Association of Independent Travel Agencies)
c/o ABTA.

AGCAS (Association of Graduate Careers Advisory Services)
c/o University of Sheffield Careers Service, 8 Favell Road, Sheffield S3 7QX, Web site: www.agcas.org.uk

AITO (Association of Independent Tour Operators)
133a St Margaret's Road, Twickenham TW1 1RG, Tel: 020 8744 9280,
Web site: www.aito.co.uk

Association of Pleasure Craft Operators
Audley Avenue, Newport TF10 7BX, Tel: 01952 813 572, Web site:
www.canals.com

Association of Professional Tourist Guides
33 Moreland Street, London EC1V 8HA, Tel: 020 7505 3073, Web site:
www.aptg.org.uk

BASI (British Association of Snowsports Instructors)
Glenmore, Aviemore, Inverness-shire PH22 1QU, Tel: 01479 861 717,
Web site: www.basi.org.uk

BITOA (British Incoming Tour Operators' Association)
14 Leicester Place, London WC2H 7BZ, Tel: 020 7287 3217, Web site:
www.bitoa.co.uk

Bord Failte (Irish Tourist Board)
Failte Ireland, Baggot Street Bridge, Dublin 2, Tel: 1890 525 525, Web
site: www.bordfailte.ie

British Airways Recruitment
The Rivers Cranebank, PO Box 59, Hounslow TW6 2HB, Tel: 0870 608
0747, Web site: www.britishairwaysjobs.com

British Association of Leisure Parks, Piers and Attractions
Newington Causeway, London SE1 6BD, Tel: 020 7403 4455, Web site:
www.balppa.org

British Holiday and Home Parks Association
6 Pullman Court, Great West Road, Gloucester GL1 3ND, Web site:
www.bhhpa.org.uk

British Institute of Innkeeping
80 Park Street, Camberley GU15 3PT, Tel: 01276 684 449, Web site:
www.bii.org

CACHE (Council for Awards in Children's Care and Education)
8 Chequers Street, St Albans AL21 3XZ, Tel: 01727 847 636, Web site:
www.cache.org.uk

Career Development Loans Tel: 0800 585 505

CARTA (Campaign for Real Travel Agents)
66 Essex Road, London N1 8LR, Tel: 020 8744 9271, Web site:
www.realholidays.co.uk

CERT (Irish State Tourism Agency) Tel: 01 602 4000, Web site: www.failteireland.ie. See also Bord Failte.

Chartered Institute of Journalists
2 Dock Offices, Surrey Quays Road, London SE16 2XU, Tel: 020 7252 1187, Web site: www.ioj.co.uk

CILT (Centre for Information on Language Teaching)
20 Bedfordbury, London WC2N 4LB, Tel: 020 7379 5101, Web site: www.cilt.org.uk

CIMTIG (Chartered Institute Marketing Travel Industry Group)
Home Cottage, Old Lane, Tatsfield, Nr Westerham TN16 2LN, Tel: 01957 7460, Web site: www.cimtig.org

Civil Aviation Authority
45 Kingsway, London WC2B 6TE, Tel: 0207 379 7311, Web site: www.caa.co.uk

Confederation of Road Passenger Transport
15 Kingsway, London WC2B 6UN, Tel: 020 7240 3131, Web site: www.cpt-uk.org

Confederation of Tourism, Hotel and Catering Management
118–120 Great Titchfield Street, London W1W 6SS, Tel: 020 7612 0170, Web site: www.cthcm.com

Corporate Hospitality Association
Ferndene House, Windsor Walk, Weybridge KT13 9AP, Tel: 01932 831 441, Web site: www.cha-online.co.uk

Council for National Parks
246 Lavender Hill, London SW11 1LJ, Tel: 020 7924 4077, Web site: www.cnp.org.uk

Countryside Commission
John Dower House, Crescent Place, Cheltenham GL50 3RA, Tel: 01242 521 351, Web site: www.countryside.gov.uk

English Heritage
PO Box 569, Swindon SN2 2YP, Tel: 0870 333 1181, Web site: www.english-heritage.org.uk

English Nature
North Minster House, Peterborough PE1 1UA, Tel: 01733 455 000, Web site: www.english-nature.org.uk

Environment Council
212 High Holborn, London WC1V 7BF, Tel: 020 7836 2626, Web site: www.the-environment-council.org.uk

Farm Stay UK
NAC, Stoneleigh Park, Warwickshire CV8 2LG, Tel: 024 7669 6909,
Web site: www.farmstayuk.co.uk

Forestry Commission
231 Corstorphine Road, Edinburgh EH12 7AT, Tel: 0131 334 0303, Web site:
www.forestry.gov.uk

GBTA (Guild of Business Travel Agents)
Artillery House, Artillery Row, London SW1P 1RT, Tel: 020 7222 2744,
Web site: www.gbta-guild.com

Green Globe
GPO Box 371, Canberra, ACT 2612, Australia, Tel: +61 (2) 6 257 9102,
Web site: www.greenglobe21.com

Guild of Registered Tourist Guides
52d Borough High Street, London SE1 1XN, Tel: 020 7403 1115, Web site:
www.blue-badge.org.uk

Hospitality Training Foundation
International House, High Street, Ealing, London W5 5DB, Tel: 0208
579 2400, Web site: www.htf.org.uk

Hospitality Training Foundation – Scotland/Wales/Northern Ireland
28 Castle Street, Edinburgh EH2 2HT, Tel: 0131 124 4040, Web site:
www.htf.org.uk

Hotel, Catering and Institutional Management Association
34 West Street, Sutton SM1 1SH, Tel: 020 8661 4927, Web site:
www.hcima.org.uk

IATA (International Air Transport Association)
Central House, Lampton Road, Hounslow TW3 1HY, Tel: 020 8607 6262,
Web site: www.iata.org

Institute of Leisure and Amenity Management
ILAM House, Lower Basildon RG8 9NE, Tel: 01491 874 800, Web site:
www.ilam.co.uk

Institute of Logistics and Transport
Elstrees Court, Elstrees Road, Corby NN17 4AX, Tel: 01536 740 107, Web
site: www.iolt.org.uk

Institute of Sport and Recreational Management
Loughborough University, Loughborough LE11 3TU, Tel: 01509 226 474,
Web site: www.isrm.co.uk

International Association of Professional Congress Organizers
42 Canham Road, London W3 7SR, Tel: 020 8749 6171, Web site:
www.iapco.org

International Committee for Museum Training
City University, Northampton Square, London EC1V 0HB, Tel: 020 7040 5060, Web site: www.city.ac.uk

International Eco-Tourism Society
733 15th Street NW, Suite 1000, Washington, DC 20005, USA, Tel: +1 202 347 9203, Web site: www.ecotourism.org

Irish Travel Agents Association
32 South William Street, Dublin 2, Tel: +353 01679 4179, Web site: www.itaa.ie.

Local Government Management Board
76 Turnmill Street, London EC1M 5LG, Tel: 020 7296 6600, Web site: www.lgmb.gov.uk

National Council for the Training of Journalists
Latton Bush Centre, Southern Way, Harlow CM18 7BL, Tel: 01279 430 009, Web site: www.nctj.com

National Trust
PO Box 39, Bromley BR1 3XL, Tel: 0870 458 4000, Web site: www.nationaltrust.org

National Trust Scotland
28 Charlotte Square, Edinburgh EH2 4ET, Tel: 0131 243 9300, Web site: www.nts.org.uk

Northern Ireland Tourist Board
59 North Street, Belfast BT1 1NB, Tel: 028 9023 1221, Web site: www.discovernorthernireland.com

Qualifications and Curriculum Authority
83 Piccadilly, London W1J 8QA, Tel: 020 7509 5555, Web site: www.qca.org.uk

Pan Aviation Training Services
Tel: 020 7371 8731, e-mail: panaviation@yahoo.com

Passenger Shipping Association
288 Regent Street, London W1R 5HE, Tel: 020 7436 2449, Web site: www.psa-psara.org.

RADAR (Royal Association for Disability and Rehabilitation)
12 City Forum, 250 City Road, London EC1V 8AF, Tel: 0207 250 3222, Web site: www.radar.org.uk

Royal Geographical Society
1 Kensington Gore, London SW7 2AR, Tel: 020 7591 3000, Web site: www.rgs.org

Sports Council
Victoria House, Bloomsbury Square, London WC1B 4SE, 020 7273 1500, Web site: www.sportengland.org. Regional centres: Sport Northern Ireland, Web site: www.sportscouncil.ni.org.uk; Sport Scotland, Web site: www.sportscotland.org.uk; Sports Council Wales, Web site: www.sports-council-wales.co.uk. See local phone books for telephone contacts.

Springboard
3 Denmark Street, London WC2H 8LP, Tel: 020 7497 8654, Web site: www.springboarduk.co.uk. Information and job centre for hospitality, with some details on travel and tourism.

Swiss National Tourist Office
10 Wardour Street, London W1D 6QF, Tel: 0800 100 200 30, Web site: www.myswitzerland.com. For advice on hotel schools.

TTENTO
c/o Hospitality Training Foundation, Tel: 01932 345 835, Web site: www.spinet.co.uk

Tourism Society
1 Queen Victoria Terrace, Sovereign Court, London E1W 3HA, Tel: 020 7488 2789, e-mail flo@tourismsociety.org, Web site: www.tourismsociety.org

Tourism Training Organisation, Tel: 0906 553 2056 (calls cost £1 per minute), Web site: www.tourismtraining.biz. Private company with information helpline for jobs and training.

Travel Training Company
Tel: 01483 727 321 Web site: www.ttctraining.co.uk

UCAS (Universities and Colleges Admissions Service)
PO Box 28, Cheltenham GL52 3LZ, Tel: 01242 222 444, Web site: www.ucas.ac.uk. Information on over 1,250 tourism courses.

University of Surrey
Guildford GU2 7XH, Tel: 01483 300 800, Web site: www.surrey.ac.uk

VisitBritain
Tel: 020 8846 9000, Web site: www.visitbritain.com

Regional tourist boards

Cumbria Tourist Board
Ashleigh, Holly Road
Windermere LA23 2AQ
Tel: 01539 444 444
Web site: www.golakes.co.uk

East of England Tourist Board
Toppesfield Hall
Hadleigh IP7 5DN
Tel: 01473 822 922
Web site: www.eastofenglandtouristboard.com

England's North Country
Swan House
Swan Meadow Road
Wigan Pier WN3 5BB
Tel: 01942 510 604
Web site: www.visitenc.com

Guernsey Tourism
PO Box 23
St Peter Port GY1 3AN
Tel: 01481 726 611
Web site: www.guernseytouristboard.com

Isle of Man Tourism
Sea Terminal Buildings
Douglas IM1 2RG
Tel: 01624 686 801
Web site: www.visitisleofman.com

Jersey Tourism
Liberation Square
St Helier JE1 1BB
Tel: 01534 500 700
Web site: www.jersey.com

North West Tourist Board
Swan House
Swan Meadow Road
Wigan Pier WN3 5BB
Tel: 01942 821 222
Web site: www.nwtourism.net

Northumbria Tourist Board
Aykley Heads
Durham DH1 5UX
Tel: 0191 375 3000
Web site: www.e-northumbria.net

South West Tourism
Woodwater Park
Pynes Hill
Rydon Lane

Exeter EX2 5WT
Tel: 0870 442 0830
Web site: www.swtourism.co.uk

Tourism South East – East
The Old Brew House
Warwick Park
Tunbridge Wells TN2 5TU
Tel: 01892 540 766
Web site: www.tourismsoutheast.com

Tourism South East – West
40 Chamberlayne Road
Eastleigh SO5 5JH
Tel: 02380 625 400
Web site: www.southerntb.co.uk

Visit Heart of England
Woodside
Larkhill Road
Worcester WR5 2EZ
Tel: 01905 761 100
Web site: www.hetb.co.uk

Visit London Business and Conventions
1 Warwick Row
Victoria
London SW1E 5ER
Tel: 020 7932 2000
Web site: www.visitlondon.com

Yorkshire Tourist Board
312 Tadcaster Road
York YO2 2HY
Tel: 01904 707 961
Web site: www.yorkshiretouristboard.net

FURTHER READING

Magazines

Attractions Management, Web site: www.leisuremedia.co.uk
Careerscope, Tel: 01276 211 88
Caterer and Hotelkeeper, Tel: 01444 445 566, Web site:
   www.caterer-online.com
Coach Monthly, Tel: 01454 313 128

Conference and Incentive Travel, Web site: www.citimagazine.com

Exhibition Bulletin, Tel: 020 8971 8282, Web site: www.mashmedia.met

Group Travel Organizer, Tel: 0845 166 8131, Web site: www.grouptravelorganiser.com

Incentive Travel and Corporate Meetings, Tel: 0118 979 3277, Web site: www.incentivetravel.co.uk

Leisure Management, Tel: 01491 874222, Web site: www.leisuremedia.co.uk

Travelmole (online news), Web site: www.travelmole.com/news

Travel GBI, Tel: 020 7729 5171 (deals with tour operations in the UK and Ireland)

Travel Trade Gazette and *Travel Weekly* (can usually be found in libraries)

Travel and tourism books

Becoming a Tour Guide, Continuum, ISBN: 0 8264 4788 0

Careers in Airlines and Airports, Verite Reilly Collins, Kogan Page, ISBN: 0 749 437022

Careers in Catering, Hotel Administration and Management, Russell Joseph, Kogan Page, ISBN: 0 7494 3149 0

Leisure and Tourism Intermediate GNVQ Textbook, Pearson, ISBN: 0 582 278414

Working on Cruise Ships, Sandra Bow, Vacation Work Publications, ISBN: 1 854 582925

Press and PR guides

Hollis Press and PR Guide, 7 High Street, Teddington TW11 8EL, Web site: www.hollis-pr.com

Willings Press Guide, Tel: 01494 797 225, Web site: www.willingpress.com

Kogan Page testing and job search books

Testing books

Aptitude, Personality and Motivation Tests, Jim Barrett, ISBN: 0 7494 4178 9

The Aptitude Test Workbook, Jim Barrett, ISBN: 0 7494 3788 X

How to Pass Numerical Reasoning Tests, Heidi Smith, ISBN: 0 7494 3958 0

IQ and Psychometric Tests, Philip Carter, ISBN: 0 7494 4118 6

The Times Book of IQ Tests – Book 3, Ken Russell and Phillip Carter, ISBN: 0 7494 3959 9

Kogan Page job search aids

Great Answers to Tough Interview Questions, Martin John Yate, ISBN: 0 7494 3552 6

How You Can Get That Job!, Rebecca Corfield, ISBN: 0 7494 3894 0

Net that Job! Using the World Wide Web to develop Your Career and Find Work, Irene Krechowiecka, ISBN: 0 7494 3314 0
Preparing Your Own CV, Rebecca Corfield, ISBN: 0 7494 3839 2
Readymade Job Search Letters, Lyn Williams, ISBN: 0 7494 3322 1
Successful Interview Skills, Rebecca Corfield, ISBN: 0 7494 3892 4

Kogan Page guides to working at home

A Guide to Working for Yourself, Godfrey Golzen and Jonathan Reuvid, ISBN: 0 7494 4029 5
Running a Home-based Business, Diane Baker, ISBN: 0 7494 3682 4

For more information on Kogan Page publications visit www.kogan-page.co.uk.

Appendix

Recruitment tests

Recruitment tests are an increasingly popular part of the job interview within the travel industry. Psychometric, aptitude and IQ tests and personality questionnaires are common. The testing is designed to highlight potential skills and to identify an individual's attributes. For example, British Airways carries out verbal and numerical reasoning tests on applicants.

There are a number of ways in which an applicant can prepare for recruitment tests. Online practice tests are now readily available as are a number of books that offer practice tests (see Chapter 14). The more the job applicant can practise the better, as there are set patterns and rules in psychometric testing that can be learnt.

The following tests are from *IQ and Psychometric Tests*, Philip Carter (Kogan Page, £8.00, ISBN 0 7494 4118 6) and offer examples of numerical and verbal reasoning tests that are similar to ones that a job applicant might be asked to do.

VERBAL REASONING

Verbal intelligence tests

Test 1: Synonym test

A synonym is a word that has the same meaning as, or a very similar meaning to, another word. Examples of synonyms are: calm and placid, error and mistake, select and choose. This test is a series of 20 questions designed to test your knowledge of language and your ability to identify quickly words that have the same or very similar meanings.

You have 30 minutes to complete the 20 questions. You should work as quickly as possible as some questions will take more time to solve than others.

Questions 1 to 5

In the following five questions select the word in brackets that means the same or has the closest meaning to the word in capitals.

1. BRUSQUE (crude, curt, unkind, elastic, wieldy)

2. DISTIL (reduce, liquefy, soften, purify, rarefy)

3. SINGULAR (remarkable, free, routine, natural, upright)

4. FASTIDIOUS (chic, loyal, protective, choosy, viable)

5. WAX (souse, fade, shrink, strengthen, dilate)

Questions 6 to 10

In the following five questions, from the six words given identify the two words that you believe to be closest in meaning.

6. flawless, ulterior, unwelcome, secret, overt, literate

7. circle, row, pedal, track, flaw, line

8. relative, common, exoteric, indolent, careless, apposite

9. ascribe, profess, aspire, judge, hanker, daze

10. vote, composite, blend, proposition, element, total

Questions 11 to 20

The following are a miscellaneous selection of question types where, in each case, you have to identify two words with similar meanings. Read the instructions to each question carefully.

11. Complete the two words, one in each circle and both reading clockwise, which are similar in meaning. You have to find the starting point and provide the missing letters.

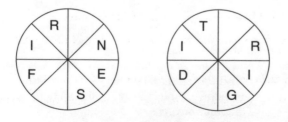

12. Complete the two words, one in each circle and both reading clockwise, which are similar in meaning. You have to find the starting point and provide the missing letters.

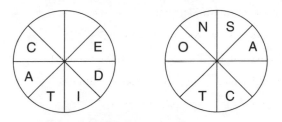

13. Complete the two words, one in each circle, one reading clockwise and the other anti-clockwise, that are similar in meaning. You have to find the starting point and provide the missing letters, and work out which word is clockwise and which is anti-clockwise.

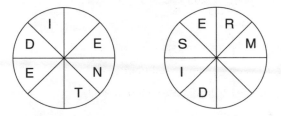

14. Which two words below are most similar to the phrase 'get the wrong idea'?

    misconceive, miscalculate, misconstrue, misinform, misapply, misconduct

15. Which two words below are most similar to the phrase 'put in a good word for'?

    conciliate, recommend, pacify, advise, endorse, enliven

16. Which two words below are most similar to the phrase 'down-to-earth'?

    subservient, dismayed, practical, earthward, explicit, realistic

17. ROPE OF CREW is an anagram of which two words (5, 5 letters) that are similar in meaning?

18. VINCIBLE OIL is an anagram of which two words (4, 7 letters) that are similar in meaning?

19. Each square contains the letters of a nine-letter word. Find the two words, one in each square, that are similar in meaning:

N	M	O		
U	E	G		
O	O	L	L	O
		Y	U	O
		Q	S	I

20. The circles contain the letters of two eight-letter words which can be found reading clockwise. Find the two words, which are similar in meaning. Each word starts in a different circle, and all letters appear in the correct order and are used once only.

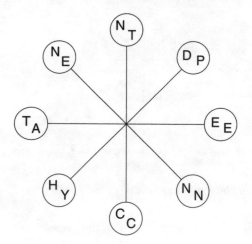

Answers to Test 1

1. curt

2. purify

3. remarkable

4. choosy

5. dilate

6. ulterior, secret

7. row, line

8. relative, apposite

9. aspire, hanker

10. composite, blend

11. firmness, rigidity

12. accredit, sanction

13. sediment, residuum

14. misconceive, misconstrue

15. recommend, endorse

16. practical, realistic

17. power, force

18. bill, invoice

19. monologue, soliloquy

20. tendency, penchant

Assessment

Each correct answer scores one point.

8–10	Average
11–13	Good
14–16	Very good
17–20	Exceptional

NUMERICAL REASONING

Numerical calculation and logic

As well as diagrammatic tests, numerical tests are regarded as being culture-fair to a great extent, as numbers are international. In addition to testing your powers of calculation, many of the tests also test your powers of logic, and your ability to deal with problems in a structured and analytical way.

We all require some numerical skills in our lives, whether it is to calculate our weekly shopping bill or to budget how to use our monthly income. Anyone who has ever taken an IQ test will be familiar with the types of numerical tests encountered, and the flexibility of thought and often lateral thinking processes needed to solve them. The more one practises on these types of little puzzles, the more proficient one becomes at solving them.

Test 1: Calculation and logic A

This test is a battery of 15 number puzzles designed to test your numerical ability. You have 60 minutes in which to solve the 15 puzzles. The use of a calculator is permitted in this test.

1. What number should replace the question mark to continue the sequence?

    1, 5, 13, 29, ?

2. How many minutes is it before 12 noon if 40 minutes ago it was four times as many minutes past 10 am?

3. What number should replace the question mark?

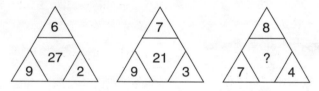

4. What number should replace the question mark to continue the sequence?

    100, 96.5, 92, 86.5, ?

5. What value of weight should be placed on the scales to balance?

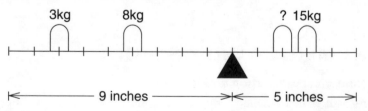

6. Tony and Cherie share a certain sum of money in the ratio 2 : 5. If Cherie has £195.00, how much money is shared?

7. Insert the numbers 1, 2, 3 , 4, 5 into the circles, one per circle, so that:

    the sum of the numbers 2 and 1, and all the numbers in between
    is 7

    the sum of the numbers 2 and 3, and all the numbers in between
    is 10

    the sum of the numbers 5 and 3, and all the number in between
    is 15

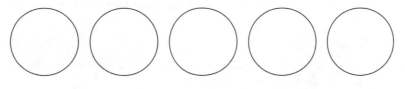

8. What is the difference between the sum (added together) of the
    largest two odd numbers in grid A and the product (multiplied
    together) of the smallest two even numbers in grid B?

A

17	14	9	5
11	24	19	18
12	13	10	7
23	28	15	16

5	20	7	18
22	32	24	4
26	14	23	36
9	21	16	15

B

9. What two numbers should replace the question marks to continue
    the sequence?

    1, 10, 2.75, 8.25, 4.5, 6.5, 6.25, ?, ?

10. If Peter's age + Paul's age = 39
    and Peter's age + Mary's age = 44
    and Paul's age + Mary's age = 47
    how old are Peter, Paul and Mary?

11. What numbers should replace the question marks?

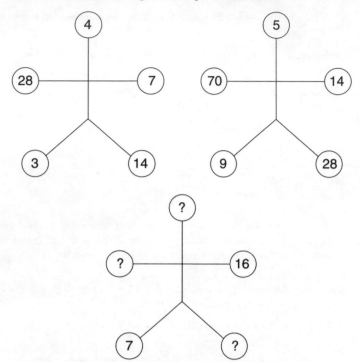

12. What is 3/11 divided by 18/44 to the smallest fraction?

13. What number should replace the question mark?

2	7	10	15
5	10	13	18
10	15	?	23
13	18	21	26

14. What number should replace the question mark to continue the sequence?

17, 34, 51, 68, ?, 102

15. What number should replace the question mark?

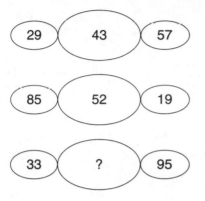

Answers to Test 1

1. 61: add 4, 8, 16, 32.

2. 16 minutes: 12 noon less 16 minutes = 11.44. 11.44 less 40 minutes = 11.04. 11.04 less 64 minutes (4 × 16) = 10 am.

3. 14: 8 × 7 = 56; 56/4 = 14. Similarly 7 × 9 = 63; 63/3 = 21.

4. 80: less 3.5, 4.5, 5.5, 6.5.

5. 4 kg

    4 × 8 = 32   3 × 15 = 45

    7 × 3 = 21   2 × 4 = 8

    ---53---   ---53---

6. £273.00. Each share is 273/7 (2 + 5) = £39.00. Therefore Cherie's share is 5 × 39 = 195 and Tony's share is 2 × 39 = 78.

7. 5 2 4 1 3 or 3 1 4 2 5

8. 14: A = 19 + 23 = 42 and B = 4 × 14 = 56.

9. 4.75, 8. There are two alternate sequences, one starting at 1 and adding 1.75, and the other starting at 10 and deducting 1.75.

10. Peter 18, Paul 21, Mary 26.

11. A + C = E, A × E = B, A + E + C = D.

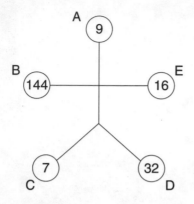

12. 2/3

3(1)/11(1) × 44(4)/18(6) = 2/3

13. 18. Looking across each line add 5 and 3 alternately. Looking down each column add 3 and 5 alternately.

14. 85: add 17 each time.

15. 64: (33 + 95)/2. Similarly (29 + 57)/2.

Assessment
Each correct answer scores one point.

6–7	Average
8–9	Good
10–13	Very good
14–15	Exceptional

Index